Living Simply

Living Simply

AN EXAMINATION
OF CHRISTIAN LIFESTYLES

Edited by David Crean
and Eric and Helen Ebbeson

THE SEABURY PRESS / NEW YORK

Life goes wrong when the control of space,
the acquisition of things of space,
becomes our sole concern

—*Rabbi Abraham Joshua Heschel*

Second printing
1981
The Seabury Press
815 Second Avenue
New York, N.Y. 10017

Library of Congress Cataloging in Publication Data

Living simply.
1. Christian life—Anglican authors.
2. Simplicity. I. Crean, David. II. Ebbeson, Eric.
III. Ebbeson, Helen.
BV501.2.L595   248.4'83   81-5834
ISBN 0-8164-2340-7   AACR2

Note to the Reader
All biblical references are to the Revised Standard
Version of the Bible. Old Testament Section, copyright ©
1952; New Testament Section, First Edition, copyright ©
1946; Second Edition © 1971 by Division of Christian
Education of the National Council of Churches of
Christ in the United States of America.

Grateful acknowledgment is made for the use of the following materials:
"Responses to Change: Goodbye More—Hello Less,"
copyright © 1980 by David Dodson-Gray is reprinted by
permission of the author.
"Shalom: Toward a Vision of Human Wholeness,"
copyright © 1980 by Bruce C. Birch is reprinted from *Response*,
Journal of the United Methodist Churchwomen, by permission of
that organization and the author.
Lines from "Choruses from 'The Rock' " by T.S. Eliot are
reproduced by permission of Harcourt Brace Jovanovich, Inc.
from COLLECTED POEMS 1909-1962 by T.S. Eliot, copyright 1936
by Harcourt Brace Jovanovich, Inc.; Copyright © 1963, 1964 by T.S. Eliot.

Contents

Foreword

In 1979, the Sixty-Sixth General Convention of the Episcopal Church resolved that

> . . . every member of this church exercise a responsible life style based on real personal needs commensurate with a world of limited resources.

This book is, essentially, a response to that call. It does not show people *how* to change lifestyle. That would be impertinent. It does try to put the imperative that we should change our overconsumptive lifestyles in the theological context of stewardship—stewardship of the resources that feed, clothe, and warm us on a small planet. We hope that those reading this book will be encouraged to make changes, and to facilitate this we refer them to the resources in the final chapter ("And Furthermore . . .").

It was our original concept that this would not be a book to be read as one would read a novel. It is designed for small group study. This stems from our premise that lifestyle changes, to be effective, should take place in a support community. It is thus designed for study and discussion.

An undertaking such as compiling this book is not accomplished without the support of a large number of people. We thank the Presiding Bishop, the Right Reverend John M. Allin, and Mrs. Alice P. Emery, Executive for National Mission in Church and Society, for their support. The National Hunger Committee under the chairmanship of the Reverend J. Fletcher Lowe, Jr. has provided valuable guidance.

We owe a particular debt of gratitude to Mr. Gary Evans, who compiled the questions accompanying each chapter as well as the biblical reflections, and Dr. David V. Williams, who helped focus our thinking and gave us more good ideas than we could possibly use. We also thank the Reverend Charles A. Cesaretti for his valuable input and encouragement, and the Reverend R.B. Lloyd and the Social Ministries Committee of the Appalachian People's Service Organization for helping focus our thoughts on lifestyles.

Without the dedicated skill of Ms. Janet E. Vetter who typed and retyped the manuscript, we would never have made the deadline. We also thank Mrs. Joyce Glover for her editorial assistance.

To our authors belong our undying thanks. Such errors as exist are our responsibility; the virtues of the book are entirely theirs.

The Editors

Introduction

Lifestyle.

It's one of those words. Everyone knows what it means; but just try to define it! The word is so new that it does not even appear in many dictionaries published as recently as the 1970s.

Some think of lifestyle in geographic terms—one kind for California, another kind for the Northeast, and so on.

Others associate lifestyle with different chronological ages—one for youth and another that is peculiar to their retired grandparents.

Some connect lifestyle with a person's attitude toward sex—sexual permissiveness on the one hand and sex limited to marriage on the other.

This book, however, treats the concept of lifestyle in a way that cuts across these other ways of thinking. Whether one be old or young, urban or rural, an Easterner or a Westerner, one must come to terms with a style of personal life that relates—more responsibly or less responsibly—to everything else and everyone else on this planet. Consciously or unconsciously I live my daily life on the basis of certain assumptions that I make about the world around me—about my fellow human beings on this and other continents; about living things, "beast, bird or fish," that also live on this planet; and about the air and the water and all the inanimate things that help to make this world habitable.

These assumptions have a great deal to do with the way I consume energy and food, the forms of human community with which I feel comfortable, and the way I relate my life to those I love and to those in far places whom I will never see.

On the one hand these assumptions lead me to act as I do each day and to make the choices I make, thus determining my lifestyle. On the other hand these assumptions, if I take the trouble to examine them, show me what I *really* believe about the purpose of my life and the purpose of the Creator who made my life possible.

If these assumptions are that important, it makes sense to take a close look at them and to test them against the assumptions of saints and scholars who have lived before us—and those who are our contemporaries. This book is written to help us in this examination.

I have a feeling that most people don't exert themselves a great deal to examine the assumptions underlying their lifestyles until they are confronted with some startling but inescapable fact.

One person's assumptions about food consumption may be shattered by a Frances Moore Lappé. She points out that, in a world where millions starve, we in the United States feed 78 percent of all our grain to animals and in the process feed 20 million tons of protein a year to livestock in order to retrieve only 2 million tons of protein in meat for human consumption. The 18 million tons of protein that are thus wasted each year are enough, she says, to overcome 90 percent of the world's protein deficiency—enough to provide 12 grams of protein a day to every person in the world.

As for me, it was my assumption about world supplies of energy that was first challenged. About ten years ago I realized that I could no longer live as though there would always be more and more energy available for a lifestyle that required more energy for more gadgets, bigger cars, and energy-wasteful homes. I realized that there was just so much oil, coal, and natural gas in the earth, and nobody was down there making any more of it. Some day, sooner or later, it would be exhausted. If sooner, humankind would be hard pressed to find alternate, renewable forms of energy in time to prevent worldwide economic and social chaos. If later, we just might have time (I reasoned) to make the switch to renewable forms of energy without such disruption.

By reading and adapting what was already in print I was able to build a simple solar water heater from "junkyard" parts, a solar greenhouse, and a solar space heater on our 80-year-old home. I did it partly to save money and partly to give the lie to those who kept insisting that solar energy would be impractical for decades to come. But in doing it I found that I was "backing into" a new reverence for energy conservation. I was going to make sure that those precious

BTU's (heat-energy units) which I had labored so hard to extract from the sun were not going to leak easily out of my home. And I became aware that a BTU conserved was the equivalent of a BTU that would never have to be extracted from any oil well or coal mine. I began publicizing the finding of the American Institute of Architects that conservation measures *in buildings alone* would save more energy each year than is contained in all the oil produced each year in the United States, including the Alaskan pipeline.[2] Every conserved BTU can therefore buy more time for the world to make the transition to a sustainable society.

The Joint Strategy and Action Committee, Inc. (JSAC), which I have the privilege of serving, decided several years ago to establish a new task force dealing with lifestyle. There had been for some years a JSAC Alternate Lifestyle Work Group. But the connotation was that it was only for a few eccentric environmentalists on the fringes of society. We decided that it was time for a new task force to help church people understand that a simpler lifestyle should now be the norm for *everyone,* and we had about decided to call it the Simple Lifestyle Task Force. But a sage on our Board of Directors said, "It seems to me that to live simply is important but not enough; some people retreat to rural communes in order to live simply and forget about the rest of the world. Why not call it the Responsible Lifestyle Task Force?" And we did!

At a recent meeting of this task force someone said, "It is not enough to live simply and responsibly. We must live *faithfully* to the God who calls us to serve Christ in the service of all humankind." And so we must.

Lifestyle.
One that is an alternative to unthinking consumption, yes.
One that is simple, to be sure.
One that is responsible and caring for all the world, of course.
And, finally, one that is faithful, with a sense of stewardship to God and to Him who came "that we might have life and have it more abundantly."

John C. DeBoer

SECTION ONE

BIBLICAL REFLECTION

Humanity as Community
by Gary T. Evans

And you shall make response before the Lord your God, "A wandering Aramean was my father; and he went down into Egypt and sojourned there, few in number; and there he became a nation, great, mighty, and populous. And the Egyptians treated us harshly, and afflicted us, and laid upon us hard bondage. Then we cried to the Lord the God of our fathers, and the Lord heard our voice, and saw our affliction, our toil, and our oppression; and the Lord brought us out of Egypt with a mighty hand and an outstretched arm, with great terror, with signs and wonders; and he brought us into this place and gave us this land, a land flowing with milk and honey. And behold, now I bring the first of the fruit of the ground, which thou, O Lord, hast given me." And you shall set it down before the Lord your God, and worship before the Lord your God; and you shall rejoice in all the good which the Lord your God has given to you and to your house, you, and the Levite, and the sojourner who is among you.

When you have finished paying all the tithe of your produce in the third year, which is the year of tithing, giving it to the Levite, the sojourner, the fatherless, and the widow, that they may eat within your towns and be filled, then you shall say before the Lord your God, "I have removed the sacred portion out of my house, and moreover I have given it to the Levite, the sojourner, the fatherless, and the widow, according to all thy commandment which thou has commanded me."

Deuteronomy 26:5 – 13

National social welfare and security programs are a familiar feature of most northern hemisphere countries today. In the United

1

States, signs of resistence, resentment, and suspicion of fraud are increasingly evident in the public attitude toward such programs.

There is no mention in Deuteronomy of public response to the cultic stipulation of a tithe of produce for the benefit of the local priest, resident aliens, orphans, and widows on every town. However, one might infer from the number of references to such concern in the text that people were not easily convinced that such behavior was their obligation.

The affirmation of faith and loyalty contained in Deuteronomy 26 makes clear the two factors to which this social obligation is related: the experience within history of a faithfully caring God, and solidarity arising from a sense of a shared human condition.

People who have experienced a remission of cancer often characterize their lives as a gift for which they are thankful every morning. In the historic memory of Israel, their free existence in a land they could call home was experienced as a gift from God who had somehow enabled their ragtag band to escape the organized might of Egypt. As the actual event receded into the past, a harvest festival was established for annually renewing the memory. It was apparently not easy to keep alive a feeling of gratitude for freedom, or for life itself.

This experience and its cultic observance also helped shape their relationship with other people. In their own history, they had experienced great material want, physical cruelty, and degrading servitude. As long as the momory of this hardship survived alongside the certainty that God had demonstrated his concern for their liberation from such circumstances, they were bound to acknowledge a solidarity with others who required freedom from "slavery" to economic circumstances. Such concern included not only kin and fellow citizens, but even sojourners, the resident aliens with no legal claim on Israel.

The historic experience of Israel led to linking of fidelity to a caring God with ethical interpersonal behavior and a just economic system. Would you agree with the assumption implicit in Deuteronomy 26 that the purpose of a community's economic structures is to supply need, with particular attention to those who are in want?

Chapter 1

Struggling for Survival

by Charlotte Fardelmann

Cowboy versus Indian is the age-old battle of the West. In South Dakota, both of these lifestyles are being threatened by a larger power, multinational energy corporations that are moving in to mine the coal, uranium, gold, and other minerals of the Black Hills, the sacred land of the Lakota (''Sioux'' to white man) Indian. An energy executive, a rancher, and an Indian express their concerns.

J. B. sits at his large desk in his office, part of his home, located in the Black Hills. His hair is graying, and he has the slight paunch of a man who has little time for exercise. On his desk are airline tickets, indicative of his frequent travels on company business.

"I like it here in South Dakota," he remarks, "but who knows, in five years I may get itchy feet." His company moved him here about a year ago to work on preliminary plans for a new uranium mine in the Black Hills.

The Lakota Indians claim ownership to the Black Hills, their *Paha Sapa,* under the Fort Laramie Treaty of 1868.

"The treaty doesn't mean anything to us," remarks J.B. "It can't. We have to deal with the legal landowner." In his opinion, the Indians need to become assimilated into the mainstream of American life. "Everyone needs help, but I can't see feeding them on a permanent basis," he says.

J.B.'s home is new, just built when he, his wife, and two children moved in. It is located in an expensive subdevelopment, and includes living room, modern kitchen, family room, office, several bedrooms, and a two-car garage. "We have three bathrooms for the four of us, and we seldom get in a bind," he says. He also remarks that he likes the comfortable lifestyle, and "isn't about to go back to the outhouse."

"The American way of life is the best in the world," he says with pride. "Our country supplies more goods to more countries than any other nation," he says, and argues the importance of mining for our way of life. It is mining and farming done by large corporations on a huge scale that makes us leaders in the world, he points out. J. B. argues that refugees from all over the world want to come to America, and he says with pride, "What you waste in a day, an African family can feed on for a week."

He talks about his background, his schooling as a mining engineer, his jobs all over the world, and his religion. "I find religion fascinating. When I lived in Arkansas, I went to Catholic Mass early in the morning, then Presbyterian church service and attended the Methodist Men's Evening Fellowship because I didn't know who had the franchise."

J.B.'s conversational style is aggressive. He defends nuclear energy and thinks we will have breeder reactors in the future. Uranium mining is under fire for exposing the water table to radioactivity and for depositing huge piles of radioactive tailings which blow in the wind and spill into the rivers.

J. B. discounts the environmentalists' concerns. "The government goes overboard in protecting people. In some places in the United States, people have been drinking water with high readings of radioactivity for years with no ill effects."

To show he is not worried about such things, he picks up his doorstop, a good-sized boulder of uranium ore and sets it on his Geiger counter. "Beep, beep, beep . . . " goes the signal. From the shelf, he takes a jar of "yellowcake," the pure uranium powder left after the milling is done. The Geiger counter goes wild. "If you are afraid of radiation, you shouldn't be in this room," he laughs. "I don't believe radiation can hurt you, at least not in small doses."

J. B. speaks about the people who are taking his company to court. "They are a thorn in our side. They are against everything, against profits, against capitalism, I can't see anything they are for."

One of those people is Marvin Kammerer, a rancher who lives an hour's drive east of J. B.'s home, on the flat land near Rapid City. The rivers from the Black Hills flow east and the rancher shares the aquifer under his land with mining corporations in the Black Hills.

Marvin Kammerer is third generation on the land, his grandfather was a "squatter" under the Homestead Act. Marvin is lean, rugged, and has eyes that look straight into your gut. His cowboy hat seems glued to his head, never coming off even as he sits in the living room. His wife holds a grandchild, and his ten-year-old son stretches out on the floor, chin in hand, to listen to his father's words.

"My grandfather raised eight children on the land, my father rasied eleven, and I'm raising seven. The land has been good to me. If I live to be a hundred, I'll never own the land. The land owns me."

He goes on, "I've never seen a man go into a box to be buried with a piece of paper in his hand that said he owned anything. We are merely occupiers, and we got to realize our time here is rather short. I have a responsibility as occupier of this land to see that when I leave it, it is in as good a shape as it was when I come on it, or better: that there is still water here safe to drink, land here to raise healthy livestock and healthy grain."

Marvin Kammerer is worried about the energy corporations moving into his area. For one thing, the water is a scarce item here, with only ten to fifteen inches of rainfall a year. According to many predictions, the proposed mining of coal, uranium, and gold scheduled to take place in the Black Hills area could easily dry up his wells. Water rights are being allocated to corporations at a rate above expected replacement from rainfall. Comments Marvin: "Wasting resources is like stealing from children that aren't yet born."

Radioactivity in the water is another concern. The tailings from an abandoned uranium mine in Edgemont, in the Black Hills, have already polluted some of the river water. Chemical pollution is another worry.

He shows me around the house. There is no central heating, only a woodstove and a propane heater. His wife sometimes complains that the house is cold, but Marvin's philosophy is, "If you're cold, put on a damn sweater."

Marvin's wife has a full-time job, and, as Marvin puts it, "the kids take up the slack." There are plenty of chores to be done, with 170 sheep, 65 beef cattle, 3 milking cows, a number of pigs, a goat,

6 horses, and 3 ponies. The younger children ride horseback three miles to school.

Marvin's nearest neighbor is ten miles away. The sheriff is thirty miles, so for all practical purposes, Marvin is his own protector.

The United States government confiscated part of his land to build Ellsworth Air Force Base, which now has the greatest concentration of land-based nuclear might of any military base in the world. The government is suing Marvin for rights to use more of his property. "Every plane that flies overhead is a daily reminder of the nuclear destruction potential we have round the world, anywhere in the world, maybe right here," he says. Marvin notes that much of the uranium mined goes to make weapons.

Western South Dakota has been suggested as a possible site for nuclear waste disposal. According to Marvin's thinking, it is "probably because the political forces are weak. The people who proposed that wouldn't want the stuff in their backyard, and they have no business asking me to take it," comments the rancher.

Marvin is disappointed by the apathy among his fellow ranchers when it comes to these issues. "Most of the ranchers are interested in money in the bank and in acquiring land," says Marvin. He thinks they will change their tune when they feel the pinch on water.

The Church is not active on the political issues. Marvin comments: "I don't think the Church is really in tune with people. In my opinion, the Church is careful not to rock the boat because there might not be as much in the kitty the next week. I would like to see the institutional churches get off their soft, comfortable stuffed chairs and start addressing social issues."

The Kammerer lifestyle is not a wealthy one, for the ranch is a minimum profit affair. Marvin has never purchased a new car or tractor, and he does the repairs on the old ones himself. He doesn't waste anything if he can help it.

He sees the Indian people on the reservation—sixty miles downstream to the northeast—as the real leaders in the land struggle. Marvin calls them the "guiding lights." The Indians have a traditional respect for the land, and they are ready to fight against further exploitation and poisoning of the land, particularly their sacred *Paha Sapa*.

Lakota Indian Mabel Ann Chasing Hawk stands at her kitchen

table preparing dinner for her family of six: her husband and herself and four children. Wiyaka (meaning *feather*), her youngest, opens the cans of commodities allocated to Indians by the government: canned pork, canned corn, applesauce, and rice.

"Sometimes the food is spoiled," says Mabel Ann. "The butter is rancid, or the corn meal has weevils that I have to pick out."

Her house is government issue as well, a lime-green "ranch" style house that looks a little out of place on that lonely stretch of prairie land known as the Cheyenne River Reservation. An outhouse stands behind, and on this cold winter night the outhouse seat is covered with a two-inch ring of newly fallen snow.

Mabel Ann scoops water out of a bucket for cooking, explaining her modern kitchen sink has no running water because someone stole the pump to the cistern. With only nine inches of rainfall all year, the cistern likely would have been dry anyway, so Mabel Ann's husband hauls water, as most of the Indians do, with a fifty-five gallon drum on the back of his pick up.

There is a water pipeline to the reservation, but most Indians cannot afford to tap in at a fee of $600. The water is used more by the white ranchers who own reservation land purchased from poverty-stricken Indians. These ranchers are a source of unrest among Indians because they do not have the same ideas about how to treat the land. The white people use pesticides and herbicides to grow cash crops, while Indian religion opposes fertilization and emphasizes the sacredness of the natural "Mother Earth."

"They are still sterilizing our women," says Mabel Ann. "Our women are modest, uptight when they have to go to the Indian Health Service and have white doctors deliver their babies. If a doctor says they need a tubal ligation (tied tubes), they don't understand what it means and sign the paper." She sees this as part of a planned genocide of her people.

On Pine Ridge Reservation just to the south, there is an abnormally high rate of spontaneous abortion among the Indian women. A recent study shows the drinking water on Pine Ridge Reservation has radioactive levels and other chemical levels above the safe limits. Since that study, the Indians have been told not to drink the water.

The house is warm, but Mabel Ann doesn't know how long they can afford to keep it that way. It is heated by a propane furnace, with a 250 gallon gas tank, very expensive to fill. The company will not deliver less than a full tank since is is a twenty mile drive. If the electricity goes off, the furnace will not run at all. Many Indians abandon these homes in winter, doubling up with relatives who have wood stoves in simpler, more primitive homes.

Next spring, the Chasing Hawks plan to build an underground home heated with a woodstove and south-facing windows. Mabel Ann's husband is on the tribal council, and the couple are community leaders, so they see their home as a model for others. The only catch is that the majority of Indians moved out of primitive homes only about twenty years ago and have been "brainwashed" into thinking the ranch houses are a step up and that "to live in an underground home means you're primitive, you're poor, you're dirty Indian."

Many Indians were jailed after the Wounded Knee uprising in South Dakota in the early 1970s. Mabel Ann speaks of the new self-respect growing among the Indian people since then, an increased spirituality, and a decline in alcoholism. Her own children are involved in Sun Dancing and as part of that religious involvement have vowed not to take alcohol or drugs. Her oldest son's Sun Dance bustle, made with feathers, hangs on the wall of the Chasing Hawk home.

Until about ten years ago, the Indians were not legally allowed to practice their religion. Sun Dancers were forbidden. A strong spirituality underlies the Indian life view, emphasizing the sacredness of Mother Earth. Mabel Ann is not interested in the competitive acquisition of money, which she considers to be greed. Although the government offered the Lakota Indians $122 million in settlement of the Fort Laramie Treaty of 1868, Mabel Ann's people refused to take the money. Even Wiyaka, at age three, can say "*Paha Sapa* not for sale."

J. B., Marvin Kammerer, and Mabel Ann Chasing Hawk are but three people living in a remote corner of South Dakota, but their lifestyles impinge upon one another in a struggle for survival that is mirrored around the world.

The wasteful rich outsider exploits the land and poisons the water of the native peoples. Fighting from a position of power, he battles in the courts for the right to do so.

The rancher, like the farmer, struggles to make a living from his land, often not even aware of what is being done to him. Although Marvin respects the Indians, many of his fellow ranchers treat the red man as a second-class citizen. The Indian sees her nation on the verge of genocide, hanging by a thread in the economic whirlwinds of the white man. She and her people are gathering forces in a desperate attempt to save their culture.

Only time will tell the results of the struggle going on now in South Dakota. By the time J.B.'s company and all the other companies have finished mining and moved off, the entire area might be barred from human habitation, due to pollution or lack of water—at worst, a radioactive desert. Hearken to the prophecy of Chief Seattle:

> Even the white man, whose God walks and talks with him as friend to friend, cannot be exempt from the common destiny.
> Whatever befalls the earth befalls the sons of the earth. Man did not weave the web of life; he is merely a strand in it. Whatever he does to the web, he does to himself. . . .One thing we know, which the white man may one day discover— our God is the same God. . . .This earth is precious to Him, and to harm the earth is to heap contempt on its Creator. . . .Continue to contaminate your bed, and you will one night suffocate in your own waste.

For Response and Reflection

• This book is about lifestyles. Which of the three lifestyles described in this chapter is closest to your own? What, if anything, interests or attracts you in the others? What, if anything, seems strange or unattractive to you in any of the three?

• Homes are expressions of lifestyles for the three families in this chapter. Take a walk through your home. Make a list of no more than ten items (excluding the structure of the building itself) which you feel essential to your well-being and contentment. Get some friends to do the same and compare lists.

• What difference might length of residence make in attitudes toward a place and its resources? How many people do you know who still live in the place where they were born? How do you answer the question: "Where is your home?"

• Responsible decisions and actions depend on reliable information. Choose a topic related to this chapter that you want to know more about. Go to the library and find books or periodicals to provide information. A group could do this "research" as a team effort.

Chapter 2

Components of Lifestyle
by Milo Shannon-Thornberry

Lifestyle: Individual and Institutional

At its most basic level, human life is organized around the acquisition of food, affection, shelter, clothing, and health care. Around these basic human needs are the basic "means" through which these needs are met: employment, transportation, education, recreation, and celebration. Lifestyle is the manner in which persons go about meeting their needs. It includes that blend of tastes, habits, and practices which characterize a person's everyday behavior and relationships.

Beyond the individual lifestyle is the collective or institutional lifestyle. When a group of people is linked together by certain focused interests and acts on a regular basis to achieve certain objectives, the collective manner in which that group works and interacts is its "institutional" lifestyle. Institutional lifestyle (whether at the family or national level), however, is not the sum of blending of all individual participants' lifestyles; institutional lifestyle is determined by the controlling interest or power of the group. Changing institutional lifestyles is the political part of the task, while changing individual lifestyles is the personal.

Home on the Range or in a Spaceship?

Kenneth Boulding has characterized ours as a "Cowboy" economy in which we were able to exploit the apparently limitless spaces and resources of an underdeveloped planet. We are now entering what Boulding calls a closed "Spaceman" economy in which the earth has become a single spaceship without unlimited reservoirs of anything either for extraction or for pollution, and in which humans have to find their place in a cyclical ecological system.[1]

The fruits of the "Cowboy" outlook are becoming clearer day by day. Albert J. Fritsch, a Jesuit priest-scientist who helped found the Center for Science in the Public Interest, well describes our situation:

> We have become fenced in and congested; our water and air is being polluted; our sources of readily available energy and protein are becoming scarce; nations are scrambling for raw materials with little regard for the needs of other nations. The developed countries gorge themselves and vomit their wastes from smokestacks and sewer pipes, while the young developing nations are turned loose and advised to scavenge for themselves.[2]

The situation Fritsch describes in the industrialized countries is being tragically repeated in many Third World countries. In Brazil, for example, the rapid and massive destruction of the world's largest rain forests—an important source of oxygen for our atmosphere—in the interest of "development" is providing a severe shock to the balance of nature because millions of acres of land are being lost to erosion, with the further prospect that world weather patterns will be altered by the absence of the forests.

The Human Cost

The change from the "Cowboy" to the "Spaceperson" perspective not only necessitates seeing the ecological balance of this planet differently, but requires seeing human relationships in a different light. Through "Cowboy" eyes, the world was viewed as a pie without limits. There were pieces for all who would work hard enough to get them. And the size of one's piece depended on the person's own efforts.

Through "Spaceperson" eyes, the size of the pie is limited. While there is enough for everyone's need, there is not enough for everyone's greed. That is, the high levels of consumption by thirty percent of the world's population are directly related to the continued impoverishment of the other seventy percent. This may be better appreciated when one understands that 30 percent of the world's population receives seventy percent of the world's income. That inequity is due less to ignorance, laziness, and lack of resources than to the fact that the "rules" of the world economic "game"—as applied to trade, the international monetary system, the operation of large multinational corporation—are "fixed" in favor of the industrialized nations of the world.

To affluent North Americans this is a difficult pill to swallow. In the first place, it is not easy to see how the ways we live adversely affect someone else. And second, it makes us feel guilty to learn that our "good life" is, to a degree, supported by someone else's poverty. Consider, for example.

—What the price of sugar would be if a living wage were paid to the cane cutters in the Dominican Republic; Or of tomatoes and oranges if adequate wages were paid to farm workers.

—What the price of televisions would be if they were not made with cheap labor in places like Taiwan and Korea.

—What the price of prescriptions might be if the pharmaceutical companies could not "dump" (sell) surplus or non-F.D.A. approved drugs in Third World countries.

How secure you would feel if you had to live near the toxic wastes produced in making the convenience gadgets in your home.

How much less the dollar might be worth than it already is if it weren't for arms sales by the United States to other countries.

What might it mean to work at changing ourselves and our society so that both care more for people and the environment? The chart below is designed to show the interrelationship between individual and institutional lifestyle change. The chart is no "formula" for responsible living. Readers will do well to be wary of any simple formula. This chart is intended only to be illustrative or suggestive.[3]

POSSIBLE LIFESTYLE CHANGES

Components:	Individual (Personal)	Institutional (Political)
Food	1. Eat less. 2. Raise and preserve your own; share with those who can't garden. 3. Eat more nutritious food, less junk and processed foods.	1. Support measures assuring access to food for everyone. 2. Advocate support of family farms and direct farmer-consumer marketing. 3. Work for equal time nutrition advertising; organize to replace junk foods in schools with good snacks.
Affection	1. Put nurturing ahead of other tasks in the home. 2. Reemphasize the values of the extended (multi-generational) family.	1. Organize at your workplace to decrease alienation between family and work (crèches for nursing mothers, child care facilities). 2. Promote measures which encourage the in-home care of the elderly, ill, retarded.
Shelter	1. Determine the amount of space you really need; share with those without shelter. 2. Weatherize your house; consider using solar energy. 3. Resist the use of materials which are not biodegradable or are made with non-renewable resources.	1. Use your church building as shelter for homeless people, daycare, and senior citizen center. 2. Support legislative measures to assist in weatherizing homes, primarily those of the poor. 3. Support environmental protection measures.
Clothing	1. Make or buy utilitarian clothes of natural fibers which are good for your body and the environment. 2. Resist the impulse to buy clothes to make you feel good or give you self-assurance.	1. Undermine expensive "dress codes" where you work or go to school. 2. Organize an "advertising awareness" group to learn more about the power and method of advertising.
Health Care	1. Treat your body with respect; emphasize preventive care.	1. Support measures which assure access for all to adequate health care.

Components:	Individual (Personal)	Institutional (Political)
	2. Breast-feed your infant if possible.	2. Support efforts opposing the promotion of infant formula among Third World people.
Employment	1. Determine to what extent your employer's policies and practices compromise your concern for the environment and people. 2. Hire persons to do work you might have done with machines.	1. Participate in stockholder actions designated to promote corporate responsibility. 2. Support measures that will provide for full, meaningful, adequately paid employment.
Transportation	1. Drive less; walk; bicycle; use mass transit more. 2. Buy smaller more fuel-efficient cars.	1. Support city, state, national efforts to provide mass transportation. 2. Support public policies encouraging use of smaller cars.
Education	1. Have children attend public schools. 2. Consider continuing-education a necessity. 3. Work at awareness of race, sex, age, and class bias in children's textbooks.	1. Organize to resist "white flight" to private schools. 2. Encourage provision of adult education with insured access for low income and other disadvantaged groups. 3. Support organized efforts to eliminate such bias from textbooks.
Recreation	1. Blend work and leisure. 2. "Get Away" closer to, or at, home.	1. Support measures which make work more meaningful in workplaces. 2. Encourage low capital, low energy recreation activities in your communities.
Celebrations	1. Celebrate the meaning of life in "rites of passage" (birthdays, weddings, funerals). 2. Celebrate with less buying and energy use.	1. Review wedding and funeral policies in your church; encourage simplicity. 2. Support efforts in your church to divert resources from celebrations to justice and earth concerns.

Changing our lifestyles is not easy. Living on a "spaceship" requires new respect for our environment and our fellow passengers. We don't know all that the new journey will require of us, but we know enough to get started. We can take some comfort from an old Chinese proverb which states, "A long journey begins with the first step." Let's begin.

For Response and Reflection

Do you see yourself as more like the "Cowboy" or the "Spaceperson" in your present attitude toward the earth, its people, and its natural resources? What, if anything, seems to be making it hard to maintain your chosen lifestyle and attitudes?

• The author of this chapter writes, ". . .it is not easy to see how the ways we live adversely effect someone else." He then gives some examples of such negative effects from his point of view (e.g., the price of commodities and products in the U.S. and the low wages paid for their production in other countries). In a group, discuss the topic, using one of the specific examples cited. You will probably need to do some research at a library to provide factual information to support your discussion.

• Reread the chart of possible personal and institutional lifestyle changes. Make the following marks beside each item: a check beside any which you are already doing; a plus beside those with which you agree; a minus next to those with which you disagree; a question mark to indicate a lack of understanding on your part; an exclamation point beside any which were new, unexpected, or exciting to you. Several people could compare their reactions.

Chapter 3

Unity, Constancy, and Peace

Liturgy and the Simple Life
by Richard A. Bower

'Tis a gift to be simple
'tis a gift to be free
'tis a gift to come down
where you ought to be.
And when you find yourself
in the place just right,
'twill be in the valley
of love and delight.

An old Shaker hymn

Most of us have times of deep longing for simplicity, longing for simpler times, for simpler lives, for simpler relationships. We long for what is simple because we long to be free, and complexity so often feels like bondage. So the old Shaker tune, "Simple Gifts" is right, we feel, when it links simplicity with freedom. It is right, too, when simplicity is seen as a gift.

This longing for freedom and this awareness of "gift" lies at the heart of the Christian life. It lies at the heart of what we mean by claiming the wonder of God as Holy Spirit. Holy Spirit, freedom, gift, simplicity: all are interwoven, one with the other.

True, the Christian tradition does not specifically speak of the Holy Spirit in terms of simplicity. Rather it uses words like fire, life, wholeness (sanctification), harmony, completion, as well as gift.

Love and harmony . . . : that is what simplicity and freedom are about, that experience of which the old Shaker song sings. The opposites of love and harmony are fragmentation, competition, alienation, fear, and the other forms of chaos we find so prevalent in our complex and warring world.

In the beginning of creation, the Holy Spirit hovered over it all, brooding over the angry waters, bringing harmony (cosmos) out of chaos. At Pentecost the disarray and fragmentation of the nations, with their multitude of tongues, were bridged by the harmonizing presence of the Spirit, reversing the human-made chaos of Babel.

Even the marriage liturgy speaks of the healing and harmonizing work of the Spirit. The presence of the Holy Spirit makes that often most chaotic of all relationships, marriage, a sacrament, a holy sign, reversing all the ancient wound of human kind:

> Make their life together a *sign* of Christ's love
> to this sinful and broken world,
> that *unity* may overcome estrangement,
> *forgiveness* heal guilt,
> and *joy* conquer despair.[1]

The Holy Spirit, God's healing and unifying (sanctifying) presence in the world, is the Spirit of simple freedom. It is of this simplicity and this freedom that Christian liturgy sings hopefully, promises so boldly, seeks to realize so daringly. The central offering of all Christian common prayer, the Holy Eucharist, is primarily the liturgy of transforming chaos into simplicity. It is the movement of the Holy Spirit sanctifying creation once again, enabling it to bear lovingly and confidently its Lord and Creator. The celebration of Holy Eucharist is incarnational action because through the Spirit once again God in Christ becomes present in and through creation, making us and all things "holy gifts" once more.

Bread and wine, simple gifts of creation, work of human hands, become for us the reconciling, nourishing Body and Blood of Christ, the Lord of creation. Grain and wine received in the reconciling presence of the Spirit make us see each other and all creation with new and sober eyes. This new vision is the beginning of our becoming free again, of embracing a life that is holy because it is simple.

Simplicity, then, is the gift to live a holy life. It is the gift to live in the deeper awareness of connectedness to others and to all creation.

It is the gift to travel lightly because accumulation of things, people, and experiences are unnecessary for our joy. In Christ all things are ours, and we belong to them. When St. Francis called the sun and moon, water and fire his sisters and brothers, he was being not so much a romantic as he was witnessing to the wholeness of life. Since we do not have to accumulate things for our survival, we are able to care for all of life rather than use it up. We are able to live freely with compassion because we do not have to be minding our possessions.

How then does liturgy speak to and enable simplicity and freedom? How do the ways Christians have gathered for song and prayer draw us into the sanctifying work of God in the Holy Spirit, the Lord and giver of life? I would like to reflect on this in three different ways: (1) on liturgy as *seeing* in a new way; (2) on liturgy as renewing the way we *relate* to the world; (3) and on liturgy as the experience of a *journey*.

Seeing in a New Way: Perception as Reality
Owen Barfield, in a remarkable essay on perceiving, speaks about the rainbow. "Look at the rainbow," he says. "While it lasts, it is, or appears to be, a great arc of many colors occupying a position out there in space . . . now, before it fades, recollect all you have ever been told about the rainbow and all its causes, and ask yourself the question, Is it really there?"[2]

That is a question about seeing. Let us also ask a question about meaning. For example, take the sun, the rain, and your eyesight. Alone, any one of these things can be either good, neutral, or even a source of pain.

The sun for one person may be a warm and pleasant delight. For another at the same instant it is a burning fire, a desert-waste kind of terror.

The rain may be seen by you as a relief from summer's long drought, a promise of lush and green life, a refreshment. For someone else it is a tragic end to work, a destruction of longed-for play, a flood carelessly sweeping away plans and dreams.

And your sight, that precious gift by which you receive and enter countless times of beauty, can lead to participation in events of shattering horror, sight of things you never can erase from memory.

The sun, the rain, our sight: alone, separated, fragmented, they stand for good or ill in ways we cannot control. But if we stand in an open field, daring to hold them all together—sun, rain, and vision—they offer the rainbow, a sign of hope and a thing of beauty. Together they become a shared promise of ecstasy, a new kind of connectedness, a new wholeness.

In the liturgy a similar thing happens. We bring together in one time and place individuals, differing wills, brokennesses, joys, indifferences, angers, sounds, colors, motion, bread, wine, memories fresh and ancient, roles, and many other things: and in gathering all these together, in the presence of the Holy Spirit, we see and experience them all in a new way. The disconnected gathering becomes for us a Real Presence, a reconciling, nourishing reality we experience, we "perceive," just as we did the rainbow.

Like perceiving the rainbow, this experience of God has its validity as *shared* experience. As solitary experience it might as well be fantasy or wishful thinking. But as a shared experience, liturgy enables us to see in new and believable ways, to relate to "the other" in new ways, to envision new kinds of connectedness, new wholeness, new value, new possibilities and hopes. All of this is gathered up in the acclamation: "Risen Lord, be known to us in the breaking of bread."[3]

This new way of seeing for Christians is the way of seeing ourselves and all of creation as being caught up in the new and risen life of Christ. Our whole bearing toward ourselves, others, and the world, then, has an entirely new meaning and value. Simplicity and freedom flow from this new way of seeing because survival and ownership give way to participation and care in our attitudes toward people and things in life. "Open our eyes to see your hand at work in the world about us . . ."[4] this is the form of new perception that leads to a new kind of living out our life.

Of Circles and Ladders

The second way the liturgy leads us to freedom and simplicity of life is through the reforming of our relationships. If we see in new ways, we also relate in new ways.

The forces that drive much of our lives are those of competition, growth, individualism, success, dominance, security, and the completion of tasks. All of these words describe energies that more often than not separate us one from another, cause us to use things and people for our ends, to accumulate that which we think will protect and enrich us, and to guard our turf, as it were, from people or forces who might rob us of what we have worked and struggled for. We live lives constantly on the verge of threat and loss. In our struggles to achieve and protect there is little room for freedom and simplicity.

Matthew Fox speaks about the possibility of turning achievement (accumulation) into compassion, the energy which draws us with care and joy into the life of God and of all creation. "Instead of a quest for compassion," Fox reminds us, Christian life has so often led us to a "quest for perfection (as) Western society has left us a quest for success."⁵ This striving for spiritual perfection is every bit as much a complicating, accumulating, competitive venture as any achievement effort in secular life. Fox cites the Hellenistic attachment of the imagery of achievement to "Jacob's Ladder" and contrasts these with images of "Sarah's Circle": compassion, dancing, celebrating, shared ecstasies, welcoming, survival of all, earth-orientation, and gentleness.

The liturgy, primarily because it is the celebration of the community before God, is the place where we can learn again to be related with joy to God, to persons, and to all creation. The visible community gathered sharing the earth's food once again, taking time to *deepen* rather than to expand, to let go as well as receive, to know unity instead of estrangement: this community finds freedom in its brokenness and wounds to be members again one of another. Liturgy is more like a circle dance than a ladder of ascent.

Liturgy provides a model of how we can live with and in the world, seeing it as the realm of God's redemption, the place where all things—animate and inanimate—are being made new, enabled to bear the life-giving presence of the Creator and Sustainer of all things "visible and invisible."

Traveling Lightly

The third way the liturgy leads us to freedom and simplicity of life is by calling us to journey, to move on rather than settle. If we can learn to see in new ways, and to relate in new ways, we can also become people who learn simplicity as pilgrims.

The pilgrim is not the settler. The pilgrim is always on the move, never quite at home in one place, but often at home anywhere. The settler values the place, the sense of having arrived, the possibility of building and accumulating, the experience of stability and security. The pilgrim, of necessity, must travel lightly; the settler, having no new worlds to conquer, finds worth in building up the world, the place he or she has.

Liturgy is a reminder to us that we are pilgrim people. The liturgy is a story teller, and stories speak of journeys, of history, of movement. The liturgy is a recital of events, great and small, events which the people of God have never tired of telling and retelling. In the telling of the story the event comes alive again. We can be caught up in the story and the journeying.

The liturgical story has to do with saving events. The Church Year gathers up these events and re-presents them to us year after year, to keep the stories alive, and to keep us alive as we connect our story with the saving story of the biblical tradition. Stories draw us into history; history leads us into the movement of time where we discover the God who is the God of history, the One who hallows our time, our stories, our journey.

Part of the sickness of modern culture is that it does not connect well with its story. Time, and its flow from past through present and into future, is not holy, but rather is forgotten in the rush to secure and provide for the present. The past is often forgotten, or little sense of connectedness with it is experienced. The future is avoided out of fear or loss of hope, and provision for the journey ahead is lost in the frantic effort to cope with today. In this context the past is seldom seen as a holy, valued memory renewing the present; nor is the future filled with hope or anticipation, nor is it something for which we choose responsibility. It is no wonder then that in our personal lives, or in national and political realms, or in terms of economy, ecology, armaments—to name a few issues—we are settlers, carving out meaning and security only out of the present, not looking backward or forward for renewal or strength.

How different are the people of God who celebrate their story together as they seek to remain pilgrims. The daily round of life is sanctified by the rule of prayer from sunrise to sunset, with ''the setting apart of certain times of the day for prayer, and frequent repetition of the songs and traditions of the community.'"⁶ The day's journey is made holy, is valued as the place where God is present, redeeming and renewing the times. The year, on the other hand, is set apart to recall the great saving events of God within history and for his people. The story is centered on Christ, yet reaches back to the many and ancient events of the Hebrews, to the sacred stories of a people journeying, always on the move.

The Old Testament image of the powerful conflict between settling and pilgrimage is that of the story of Babel. Leaving aside the story's bias for nomadic life over against the life of the city, it is nevertheless a remarkable story about freedom and simplicity. The massive building program of the Babel Tower was a sign of the arrogance of self-made security, heedless of the effects of this arrogance on people, on the earth, and on history.

Contrast this with the Abraham story, the man called with his family to venture out, not knowing where he was going. Abraham of necessity traveled lightly, kept open to the future, listened, observed, grew, was blessed. Babel was a sign of the need for ultimate control over things. Abraham was an example of open hands, of letting things flow, of trusting faith, and of faithful trust.

The liturgies we celebrate are of Abraham. They enable us to celebrate the journeys past, and to be nourished for the journey ahead. They spin out stories that we can enter and, in entering, can share in the saving events they represent. Liturgy is there not so much to fill us up for the coming weeks, but rather to help us keep our hands open, to keep us on the journey, traveling as freely and as lightly as we are able, to keep with the story and the meal so as to find joy with others in being pilgrims again.

The call to simplicity and freedom for Christians is the call to move from achievement-oriented spirituality to a life centered on a shared vision of relatedness to people and things, a relatedness of gentleness, of compassion, of belonging to one another.

The call to simplicity and freedom is a reminder that our worth comes not from the amount of our involvements, achievements, or possessions, but from the depth and care which we bring to each moment, place, and person in our lives. It is a call to cease adding things to our already overcrowded, cluttered lives, and to choose to let go so that we might be more deeply filled by God and by the whole of creation he has in love given us to share—justly, compassionately, and lovingly.

The liturgy is that wonderful waste of time, in which nothing tangible happens, no product is produced, no achievement is accomplished. In liturgy we simply are "present" to God, to each other, and to creation. And in this waiting "presence," God, who calls us to wait freely and simply, comes to be with us. He comes to help us *see* in new ways, to *relate* to his world with a new wholeness, and to help us find courage and joy to get on the *journey* again, with freedom to serve in unity, constancy, and peace.

He asks of us a very simple thing, something that the prophet Micah reminded his all too busy temple liturgists was at the heart of simple, faithful life: to do justice, to love tenderly, to walk humbly with your God (Micah 6:8).

For Response and Reflection

• This chapter begins with thoughts about simplicity. Do you ever wish for a simpler life or time? Does your wishing feel more like a movement toward a positive choice or a desire to get away?

• People often "give up something" in Lent as an act of devotion and spiritual discipline. Often this makes possible a simpler life and an ability to share more of life's time and other resources with others. Can you identify what you could "give up" that would make possible new ways of seeing and relating to others and the natural world? How hard would it be for you to turn such things loose permanently?

• Take time to read slowly and reflectively through the service of Holy Communion, including the portions of the Bible designated for a recent Sunday. Can you identify opportunities within the liturgy for: (1) new ideas about yourself or the world? (2) a heightened or new awareness about some other member of the congregation? (3) an increased concern or compassion for others, about which you might do something? (4) a greater sense of "connectedness" with God, other people, and nature? Review your answers as a way of preparing for your next worship participation. (See Exodus 12:1–14; Matthew 26:17–30; I Corinthians 11:23–26).

Chapter 4

Living in Community
by Sister Dorcas, C.S.M. and Nancy Wabshaw

As Christians we are members of the Body of Christ, bound to one another more surely than the cells of our own bodies are bound together by our life. We do not need to *search* for comunity. It *exists*.

Since Christian community has meant for me the traditional monastic life for nearly twenty years, I have used the threefold monastic vow of poverty, obedience, and chastity as the framework for examining all forms of human community. I will use the term *stewardship* for poverty and *authority* for obedience to broaden their scope and intelligibility. Charity would be the logical amplification of chastity, but since it has lost its vitality by overuse and misuse, I will take Charles Williams' breakdown of charity into chastity and courtesy to cover all human relationships.

All Christians, by virtue of their baptism, are bound to follow a Master who taught us about stewardship, authority, and charity. He taught his disciples not to lay up treasures for themselves on earth. He lived in poverty with nowhere to lay his head. He taught us charity by commanding us to love one another as he loves us. He demonstrated true authority by forgiving sins, healing the sick, casting out devils, washing his disciples' feet, and finally by laying down his life for us.

Stewardship
One does not need to look at our society very long to conclude that democracy, private ownership of goods, free enterprise, and capitalism neither restore Eden, nor produce Utopia, nor usher in the Kingdom of God on earth. I do not believe any other political, economic, or social system that men can devise can succeed either. Even the utopian communities of the last century failed even though

25

they really believed a perfect system existed which would indeed produce Eden or the Kingdom of Heaven on earth. Nevertheless, we can honestly say that some systems work better than others, and certainly some come closer to incarnating the Gospel standards than others.

It has been said that the Greek split between matter and spirit is responsible for all the ecological chaos we are presently experiencing. It has allowed us to despise matter and therefore to abuse it. There is perhaps much truth in this if we compare our attitude toward creation with that of the American Indian. To him, private ownership of land, for instance, would be as unthinkable as ownership of slaves is to us today. The native American saw the world "composed of a variety of sentient beings who were responsive socially and emotionally to the conduct of human beings."[1] Earth was their mother; sky their father. Their relationship to creation was one of love, reverence, and awe, in contrast to ours which is almost entirely exploitive. Moreover, they considered all gifts and good fortune to be manifestations of a power that resided in or was at least mediated by the world around them. Hence, ill fortune or sickness were the results of an absence of power or an attack of some other power, the remedy involved the restoration of the victim to a right relationship with the environment.

Economically, our society operates on a basis of surplus production and accumulation of wealth, a natural child, fed by ambition and greed, of our exploitive attitude toward creation. In order to maintain the system, the establishment encourages in its devotees economic independence, possessiveness, competition, distrust of one's neighbors and freedom from any burden of concern for their welfare (after all, *they* need to be self-sufficient also!), and consumerism as the means to personal as well as societal well-being.

And the rewards of the system (for those who can play it successfully)? A little (or not so little) kingdom for "me" that is mine alone to rule, and enjoy, and dispose of as I please. Independence, freedom, a share in the highest standard of living in the world around me. Perhaps it is a good thing we took "under God" out of the Pledge of Allegiance to the flag. He doesn't fit into that picture very well! And the cost of the system (everything has its price)? Isolation, loneliness, and loss of purpose and meaning in life for the winning one-sixth of humanity; poverty and starvation for the unfortunate five-sixths of the world's population, and pollution for all alike. Not to mention the violence engendered by such blatant injustice.

Communal living is one way to witness to a set of values that seems more in tune with our relatedness in the Body of Christ. To choose communal living is to reject independence and isolation in favor of interdependence and fellowship; it is to invest more time and energy in human relationships and less in material goods. Sharing living space, furniture, cars, tools, by even two or three families, reduces the cost of living, freeing individuals from the need to choose work on the basis of financial return. Household chores are not only lightened by sharing but also acquire new meaning as service to the group. Organization and sharing leave everyone with more free time to enjoy one another. And finally, the pooled ideas, talents, and experiences of a group of people allow each individual to participate in a whole that is greater than the sum of its parts. It is truly an icon of the Body of Christ.

But lest this solution seem too easy and obvious, let me hasten to say that communal living is also costly. In the end, it will cost you no less than your life. Therefore, Jesus *must* be the reason for communal living and the source of the life. No other motive or power will suffice. It is not enough to desire the benefits of communal living nor to protest the evils of American and Western society. The object is not to create a perfect society as was the aim of many nineteenth century communities, but simply to live out the Body of Christ.

Living in community requires some sort of sharing of material resources. The ways in which this works out are legion. For instance, a small group in a parish church might decide to pool all their income and become bank, insurance, and investment for one another. Another group might choose instead to share ordinary living space or buy an apartment building, a hotel, a farm.

This kind of sharing of property does not come easily to twentieth-century Americans who believe so deeply in the *rights* of the individual. I love to remember something C. S. Lewis wrote to the effect that whatever we get from God, it will certainly *not* be justice. None of us could endure it. In God's sight, how can anyone claim the *right* to own and dispose of things or even of our own bodies at a fleeting whim? "You are not your own. You were bought with a price" (I Corinthians 6:19–20). Not that God condemns private "ownership" of property, *per se*. But how strongly Jesus warns us against the lure and bondage of wealth. I can say from my own experience that it was easy to go and sell everything I had and follow the Lord at age twenty because at that time I owned nothing but the clothes I wore. I had nothing to lose. Nor was I wealthy in terms of relationships. It was easy to make a vow of "poverty," that is, to renounce forever my "right" to call anything "mine," to hold all things in common with my Sisters in Community. But to try to *maintain* that vow over twenty years has been incredibly difficult. Substitute time and success for money and property and the war is on. "But be of good cheer, I have overcome the world" (John 16:33).

It is interesting to note that in a thorough study of nineteenth and twentieth century communities, secular and religious, in this country, Rosabeth Kanter[2] found that all the "successful" communities (i.e., those that lasted more than ten years) chose an austere lifestyle, practiced common ownership of property (some even held clothes in common), and expected any money received by an individual to be turned in to the group. Perhaps contentment with a subsistence standard of living which forces people to relate to one another and to the earth is one key to the absence in American Indian society of the worst results of our own lifestyle: alienation, poverty, and pollution. If living in community can put us in a better relationship with the earth and its creatures than most of us have living alone or in single families, it can certainly bring us into deeper relationships with one another.

Chastity/Courtesy

Love demands an investment of time and energy in the beloved. Communal living is not only an excellent school in which to learn how to love, but it is also already the fruit of love which cares enough to share space and time and the adventure and journey of life. There is great joy in the sense of belonging to a group, and a new and liberating sense of security develops. The catch is, of course, that relating closely with any brother or sister is not always easy and peaceful. In community, one cannot always choose one's companions; not only may I find some of my sisters difficult to love, but I may also have to live with other problem relationships that do not involve me directly. It is in this furnace that one discovers the depths of one's commitment to community. It is here that love is transformed into forgiveness, and we begin to walk by faith rather than sight. It all depends on the depth of one's capacity to love regardless of circumstances, and that, in turn, depends on the degree to which one has experienced the love of God. When both are great, a concentration camp can become the Body of Christ. The deeper the relationships in a community, the more powerful will be the witness of the group, but also the more painful and scandalous will be any dissensions.

In addition to the joys and sorrows of ordinary relationships in a group, there is the tension between loyalty to the group and loyalty to the exclusive relationship of marriage and family. In most of the Christian communities today, communal living is organized on the "extended household" basis, one or more families sharing a house with several unrelated single people. This system has been in operation at Reba Place Fellowship in Evanston, Illinois for over twenty years. It has also been the basic structure of the community arising out of the Church of the Redeemer in Houston, Texas.

Men and women in Religious Orders, of course, have been living as celibates in Christian communities for more than fifteen hundred years (and this kind of Christian community will probably always exist), but comparatively few Christians are called this way. Since *all* Christians need the opportunity to live out their incorporation into the Body of Christ, I believe there is a very great need for small, parish-level communities made up of families and couples as well as single people. I emphasize *small* because we are finite creatures. The needs and problems of our "global village" seem so monstrous that they often paralyze our capacity even to deal with what *is* within our reach. Moreover, our need in this age of loneliness is to deepen relationships rather than increase their number, and again, our capacity for deep relationships is limited.

If it is important to limit the size of a group in order to provide the best climate for the development of good and healthy relationships, it is equally essential to provide adequate living space per person.

Authority

Abbot Benedict Reid, O.S.B., wrote in an unpublished paper on authority prepared for a Religious Superiors' Conference in 1979, "Authority is the power to create, restore, and maintain a relationship." This was the purpose of the Incarnation, and the Church is the sign of that restored relationship. Authority is a divine attribute, and Jesus is the ultimate expression of it. Authority is, in other words, the power to handle conflict, and its most common name is forgiveness. There are several areas of conflict which must be dealt with by authority.

The first of these is the conflict between man and God and man and himself. The sacrament of reconciliation and counseling with prayer are the surest channels of authority within the Body for dealing with these relationships.

Conflict arises also among members of the Body. Jesus gave detailed instructions about how to handle this, but they are difficult instructions. Communal living, with its multiplication of the intensity and number of interactions and relationships between people, greatly increases the occasions for conflict. Most Christian communities attempt to govern themselves by democratic ideals. Some even aim for consensus in decision-making. But often the sheer magnitude of conflict that can develop may drive the group to retreat behind an authoritarian structure. While this certainly is a more efficient, less painful method of operation, it tends to require too much of the leaders and too little of the followers. And Jesus did say, "You are not to be called rabbi, for you have one teacher, and you are all brothers" (Matthew 23:1−2). This is not to say that a group should have no designated leader. The group of Sisters at DeKoven Foundation where I live tried that for a couple of years following a rather unhappy period of authoritarian rule. The result was that everyone was so afraid of stepping on someone else's toes that no one took *enough* responsibility, and many balls dropped between the cracks. Outsiders also found us hard to deal with because they couldn't find a "head" to talk to. The Body was all arms and legs! In the end, we asked the Community to appoint Sister Letitia "Sister-in-Charge.'' All decisions are still made by, or at least referred to, the group within which the Sister-in-Charge is held to be first among equals. The model she holds up for us is a reflection of the Master's injunction to those who would be first: service. By serving both the Community's ministry at DeKoven and each member of the DeKoven staff (including the hired help), she has maintained not only the community here but also the larger teamwork necessary to keep the work going.

One frequent source of conflict is the split between the "doers" and the "be-ers"; between those who seek Community as an end and those who see it as means to some kind of ministry to outsiders. I believe that *balance* is the key to resolution of the problem. It takes a great deal of time and energy to maintain community, and that in itself is witness to the value we set on living the Body of Christ. One is tempted to think that the time spent "maintaining the Body" is somehow wasted; that it could and should be spent on outreach. Yet a group has a far greater capacity for outreach than any individual, and the whole is once again greater than the sum of its parts.

There is no easy solution to this dilemma. Both the achievement and the maintenance of equilibrium between the needs of the group and the needs for outreach and ministry are a difficult and delicate business. Jesus said, "I am the true vine, and my Father is the vinedresser. Every branch of mine that bears no fruit, he takes away"—the need to *do* something. He says also in the same paragraph, "As the branch cannot bear fruit by itself, unless it abides in the vine, neither can you, unless you abide in me"—the need to maintain the Body. If authority is indeed the power to create, restore, and maintain relationships, it operates in its fulness only within the Body of Christ, and it requires for its fulfillment a love the like of which the world has never known except in Christ and those whom he indwells.

"The true measure of a church, after all is said and done, is 'does it produce community?' " We are called to "demonstrate the transcendent togetherness and living sacrifice of revealed community." [3] The Body has only one law: "that you love one another as I have loved you," (John 13:34) and community is the context within which we are to learn to fulfill that law.

This brings us full circle back to our call to live out the Body of

Christ in some way in our lives. Living in community is a way to incarnate that spiritual reality and the love for one another that is at once the fundamental law of Christ's Kingdom and the sign of its presence among us.

For Response and Reflection

• What appeals to you in this chapter's description of the intentionally chosen community life? What, if anything, doesn't appeal? Are you able to say why?

• Discuss with others the author's statement: "Since *all* Christians need the opportunity to live out their incorporation into the Body of Christ, I believe there is a very great need for small, parish-level communities of families and couples as well as single people." Can you imagine ways in which this could happen in your church?

• Personal experience helps make new ideas less strange. Gain greater firsthand knowledge of the kind of community living described in the chapter. A visit to a nearby convent or monastery, or an "extended family" grouping might be arranged. Someone from such a community could come to a church group to speak. Reading a book that describes the experience of living in a closer community can also provide a feeling of being inside the experience.

SECTION TWO

BIBLICAL REFLECTION:

Individuals in Community
by Gary T. Evans

> Therefore I tell you, do not be anxious about your life, what
> you shall eat or what you shall drink, nor about your body,
> what you shall put on. Is not life more than food, and the body
> more than clothing? Look at the birds of the air: they neither
> sow nor reap nor gather into barns, and yet your heavenly
> Father feeds them. Are you not of more value than they? And
> which of you by being anxious can add one cubit to his span of
> life? And why are you anxious about clothing? Consider the
> lilies of the field, how they grow; they neither toil nor spin; yet
> I tell you, even Solomon in all his glory was not arrayed like
> one of these. But if God so clothes the grass of the field, which
> today is alive and tomorrow is thrown into the oven, will he
> not much more clothe you, O men of little faith? Therefore do
> not be anxious, saying, "What shall we eat?" or "What shall
> we drink?" or "What shall we wear?" For the Gentiles seek all
> these things; and your heavenly Father knows that you need
> them all. But seek first his kingdom and his righteousness, and
> all these things shall be yours as well.
>
> *Matthew 6:25–33*

When a magician's tricks rely on sleight of hand, the audience's
attention must be directed away from the crucial action in order to
preserve the illusion of reality. By contrast, the intention in these
verses is to shift the focus from illusion to reality.

Many in that hillside crowd undoubtedly had good cause to
wonder where the next meal or tunic would come from. The more
prosperous, one can assume, spent time fretting about how to
preserve and improve their holdings. For both groups, the temptation

33

could have been to devote excessive time and energy to the means of economic security, even to the point of existing in a constant state of anxiety and tension.

The way out of this anxious worry is implied by the question, "Isn't there more to life than assuring its material support?" The focus is shifted from the means of physical survival and temporary feelings of security to a compelling reason for being alive. First things need to be put first if the perspective on life is to be true. The answer implicit in the question is that the listeners should spend their lives discovering and making God's priorities their own. Earlier in this extended teaching in Matthew (chapter five), it is made clear that the first priority is an intimate, loving relationship with God. From that primary community would arise a hunger to see right established in personal and societal relationships. That would be a reason for living.

The credibility of such assertions depends on the reliability of the speaker, which is supported by two kinds of evidence here. First, there is the common human experience of the crowd: the providential care of flowers and birds; the fact that worrying never really changes matters; the visible anxiety of those without belief in God ("Gentiles").

The second, and perhaps more convincing evidence is in the speaker himself. He traveled lightly through life, without even an assured resting place at night (chapter eight). Still, he was confident, attractive, vibrant—clearly doing better than just surviving. His certainty that the Father had created a world in which needs can be abundantly met was based on personal experience.

"Isn't there more to life than assuring its material support?" What answer do your everyday activities give to this question?

Chapter 5

The American Dream: On Shaky Ground?

by Charlotte Fardelmann

In many ways, Aaron Babcock's life represents the typical American Dream, a career of upward mobility from farm boy to successful business executive, a devoted wife, two healthy children, a beautiful suburban home, and a summer cabin. How secure is their lifestyle?

Aaron and Pamela Babcock met me at the door of their large suburban home outside of Minneapolis. Everything in the setting said success, from Aaron's confident, decisive voice to the beautifully decorated interior of their home.

Here Aaron showed me through the downstairs with obvious pride. "The house you are in has been a dream of ours," he said, taking me into the family room where his two young daughters were watching television. Aaron, Pam, and I settled in the large living room with a thick pile, sky-blue carpet and a House Beautiful look.

Now that Aaron has his dreamhouse, his worry is hanging on to it. "I'm concerned about making enough money to live in this style. Basically, I think we've gotten there. The cabin, this house, now my problem is hanging on to them for the next two to three years. Our costs are fixed. We have borrowed a lot of money and are paying it back with ninety-cent dollars, or eighty-cent dollars. By the time it gets to 70-cent dollars, we will be in good shape."

Meanwhile, although Aaron makes close to $50,000 a year as executive in a wholesale lumber firm, his financial situation is very tight, as he puts it, "strapped." The income is going into tremendous mortgages while the Babcocks cannot afford to travel—"We have never taken a trip in eleven years of marriage"—and they cannot afford to go out to dinner—"We rarely go even to MacDonald's."

35

Their home was purchased a little over a year ago for about $100,000 and is now worth about $200,000. "We couldn't begin to buy it today," said Aaron.

Pamela watched Aaron with admiration from the other side of the room as he told about his boyhood growing up on a farm. "He's much more interesting than I am," she commented.

Aaron recalled, "In my house, we never had very many rules or restrictions; we had responsibilities, twenty-one cows who had to be milked at 4:30 A.M. After a couple of nights coming in at 3:30 A.M., you learned to get home by 10:00 P.M. of your own volition." He spoke of the harvest. "When the weather was good enough to harvest, you harvested. If you had a heavy date for Saturday night, forget it."

This is the kind of responsibility Aaron would like to give his own children, but he finds it difficult in suburban setting. Already he is worried about his children "going astray"—getting caught up in the drug scene or sucked into one of the "religious" cults.

"I like my work, but my family is number one," said Aaron. "That's what I work eleven hours a day for." While he doesn't get home until late most weekday nights, weekends are reserved for family, often at their cabin.

The family water-skis in summer, cross-country skis and snow-mobiles in winter. The youngsters take lessons in ice-skating, gymnastics, and guitar. Aaron's number one priority goal for ten years from now is to see his oldest daughter in college. While Aaron took his two girls up to kiss them goodnight, Pamela told me about her background. Growing up in a small town in Indiana and marrying young before finishing college, Pam's world is her family. "My husband, my children, my family are my joys," she said. "Sometimes I think I was born fifty years too late," said Pam. While she is in love with her husband—"I love Aaron more than the day we got married"—and wants to be a good homemaker, she feels pressure to have a career outside the home. "I am not a women's libber," she emphasized. It bothers her when people ask, "What do you want to stay home for?" or "What do you do all day?" She is plenty busy, cooking, decorating, cleaning, sewing, laundering, and driving the girls to afterschool lessons. "I want to raise my children right, to be good people and responsible adults. There will be time for me when my children are gone."

On the back burner of her mind is her goal to finish college and develop a career. "The sorriest thing I ever did in my life is not to finish college," she said. "It's a real thorn in my side, something you don't miss unless you don't have it." Pamela hopes to study for a degree in interior design and start her own decorating business when the children are older.

Aaron and Pam talked about religion. Aaron said, "I come from a very religious family. To me, religion is something from within, between you and God. I'm not going to stop anyone on the street and try to convert them." The Babcock family attends Congregational Church almost every Sunday, except in summer when they are at their cabin.

Pamela stated, "I wouldn't miss a Sunday. I would feel I had missed out on something." The social hour after the service is a good chance for Pam to meet and talk with people. Pam spoke about giving her children a proper religious training, "so they don't get messed up in some of the cults."

It all looks secure and settled, the American Dream come true. But inside, the Babcocks are churning with anxieties. They realize their lifestyle is on very shaky ground because of the economic, ecological, and political pressures of our times.

Pam remarked, "The future of family life doesn't look good. Our friends are getting divorced. Some of them don't want to keep their children. All around, I see free morality, drug use, lack of communication between parents so involved with their own lives that they don't have time for their children."

The Babcocks worry about our national defense, about our ability to win a "conventional war." They are concerned with the waste of money by the government, both within the United States on "welfare giveaways" and in foreign lands where money is stolen by corrupt leaders.

Inflation is a major concern. Aaron remarked, "Inflation is an absolute snowball nightmare. We are dependent upon oil and cannot control what the Arabs are going to do. Our standing of living will probably have to go down."

Pamela agreed, "If someone had told me eleven years ago, when we got married, that Aaron would make as much money as he does, I would have said we would be rich. But we are not rich. The money is worth less and less. It's scary."

Daughter Juli, at age ten, is worried about energy. Juli tells her mother not to waste electricity or gas. "There won't be any left when I grow up," she says. Juli watches the cost of everything spiraling up. "How much will a car cost when I grow up? Will I be able to afford one?" she asks her mother.

Pamela stated, "I see the lifestyle of the future as 'no frill!' I don't think our children will ever have a house like this one, or even like our first house. If they want a house, they will probably have to build it themselves. The finer things in life just won't be around except for the rich people."

She paused a moment, thoughtfully, "But there's nothing wrong with that either. We may just have a simpler way of life."

For Response and Reflection

• The poet, Langston Hughes, wrote, "Hold fast to dreams/ For when dreams die/ Life is a broken-winged bird." What are some of your dreams today? How do they compare with your dreams of five, ten, or fifteen years ago? If your hopes or dreams have changed, what factors outside yourself made the changes necessary? How many of your present dreams depend almost entirely on factors outside yourself for their realization?

• Look back through this chapter at each of the quoted remarks of the Babcock family members. Place a check mark beside those with which you are in basic agreement. Place a minus sign next to any with which you disagree. Compare your reactions and reasons for them with those of other people who have read the chapter.

• Do you feel that a simpler way of life means a lower standard of living? What do you feel is essential to a satisfying and worthwhile life?

Chapter 6

The Web of Being: Interdependence and Limits to Growth

by Preston Browning

A decade ago, when the "limits to growth" controversy first began, there were many who claimed that the proponents of a no-growth society were muddle-headed pessimists, doomsayers who did not fully recognize the ingenuity of the human mind in solving the problems modern technology and a consumer-oriented public were creating.

It is more difficult today to dismiss the warnings of those calling attention to an extremely imbalanced ecological system. One striking example of such warnings is the *Global 2000 Report* submitted to former President Carter in the summer of 1980. Its findings are described as "projections," not predictions. The methods of calculating conditions in the year 2000 assume no change in present population trends, land use practices, deforestation, pollution, etc. These projections are based on information accumulated over a period of years and are supported by findings of other agencies and organizations. The message of *Global 2000*, stark and unmistakable, is that the Faustian compulsion to dominate and plunder the earth can no longer serve as the major model of humanity's relationship to nature.

The costs of extravagant, wasteful consumption are social and economic as well as ecological. Consider the pressures from advertising and from peers to buy ever more "convenient" and "up--to-date" gadgets and appliances, comfortable and luxurious cars, tasty, and "excitingly new" food and drinks. The strains imposed on the family budget are immense, not to mention the strains upon relations within the family as one member competes with another for

39

a larger share of the financial resources available to all. It is small wonder that money is one of the most frequently mentioned factors in cases of marital distress and divorce.

Consumerism takes a toll upon family life and upon the emotional health of its members in direct proportion to the norms by which many Americans measure the quality of their lives. Increasingly those norms tend to be in terms of possessions acquired, rather than in the joy of shared experience.

Many Americans cannot buy from the "Great American Bazaar" because of low-paying jobs or unemployment. This often results in resentment and inferior feelings which can, and often does, lead to severe neurosis and/or violence.

Another social cost is the fast tempo of American life which tends to disrupt the natural rhythms of life. This leaves little time for simple pleasures, such as walking with friends, bird watching, group singing, or play reading. Have we perhaps forsaken emotional and spiritual fulfillment for the accumulation of everything including experience—experience accumulated but not savored?

However, I wish to concentrate principally upon ecological costs. We will look first at land use and then at water, forests, and environmental pollution to assess some of the dangers our current lifestyle poses to planetary survival.

Land

In the United States, agricultural land is disappearing at the rate of 16,000 acres every day, lost to urban sprawl, highways, and erosion. A report of the Council on Environmental Quality, released in early 1981, notes that in 1977, a windstorm removed twenty-five million tons of soil from a 373-square-mile area in California's San Joaquin Valley—all within twenty four hours.[1] Erosion accounts for half the land removed from agricultural production each year. In the western United States, a process of desertification affecting an area the size of the thirteen original colonies is now described by the Council on Environmental Quality as "severe."[2]

How can a world population numbering 6.35 billion at the end of the century (*Global 2000* projection) hope to sustain itself on an earth whose primary resource—its arable land—is disappearing at such an appalling rate?

Water

Water, too, will be in increasingly short supply as we approach the end of this century. Population increases alone will reduce per capita global water supplies by thirty five percent during the next two decades. Much of that decrease will occur in developing countries. But lest we delude ourselves in taking for granted God's gift to Americans of a rich and fruitful land, let us take warning from the signals nature gives us. During the extended dry spell of 1980–81, those of us who live in the East had just an intimation of what the western states have known for years, i.e., that water, like everything else in creation, is limited.

Today, the industrial, agricultural, and residential segments of our society are locked in a fierce struggle for rights to rapidly diminishing stocks of water west of the Mississippi. In part of Arizona, due to heavy agricultural and residential usage, water tables have dropped by as much as 450 feet; and in Southern California, both Los Angeles and San Diego are dependent upon water from lakes hundreds of miles away whose finite supplies are being reduced at an alarming rate. To the east, in Las Vegas, "so much water has been pumped out of the underground reservoirs that the land surface has dropped four feet in the last twenty years and opened up three-foot cracks in the earth."[3]

Most of the wheat and vegetable farming of the Far West depends upon irrigation, and thus as water tables drop and salt deposits left by irrigation accumulate, the amount of arable land in the United States takes another dip. An estimated 1,000 tons of water are needed to produce one ton of wheat. Such figures suggest that Americans may be forced to reconsider their wasteful eating habits and their heretofore unquestioned taste for grain-fed beef.

Even the trend of the seventies toward the Sunbelt may be reversed as cities in the West and Southwest discover the sheer impossibility of meeting growing demands upon an already severely taxed underground water supply.

Forests

As the *Global 2000 Report* and other recent studies make clear, the earth's forests are seriously endangered by humankind's reckless use of this resource. In the developing countries alone, "forty percent of the forests still remaining . . . in 1978'' will have disappeared by the end of this century. A good part of this destruction is due to the ''slash and burn'' tactics of poor, landless peasants who constantly push back the forest boundaries in seach of tillable soil. A more ominous threat may well be posed by the activities of multinational corporations, which lead to the denuding of vast forest tracts in the Philippines, Malaysia, Indonesia, West Africa, and the Amazon Valley. The destruction of the rain forests in such areas frequently results in desertification, and there are reports of immense areas of the Amazon Valley where the land lies barren and caked, a prey to wind and sun. Since the rain forests are a major source of oxygen in the earth's atmophere, their destruction portends ''what could be the biggest ecological catastrophe of the century.''[4]

Moreover, rain forests in the Brazilian interior have been the traditional winter habitat of birds which are the natural predators of insects attacking wheat and other grain crops in North America. As these rain forests decrease in size, so also does the bird population dependent upon them for winter homes—one more threat to food supplies in a world already down to a dangerously low grain reserve of sixteen percent of annual global consumption!

As one contemplates such examples of the interrelatedness of systems in nature, one is driven inexorably to conclude that the web of being remains a web only so long as it is respected and nurtured by humanity. When abused, it becomes a net, a net drawn ever more tightly around the human family, constantly threatening to crush the life of those who have sought to ignore or circumvent its principles.

The connection between vital oxygen and rainfall (climatic changes have already been noted in areas where rain forests have been destroyed) and the profligate use of wood for newsprint must somehow be made clear if necessary lifestyle changes are to be taken seriously by the citizens of the affluent industrialized countries. But how close to real catastrophe must we get before warning signals are heeded? Some observers think the answer to that question is: ''a point at which it is already too late.''

Pollution and the ''Greenhouse Effect''
Nothing demonstrates the possible truth of that assumption better than the so-called ''greenhouse effect.'' Stated simply, the

greenhouse effect results from excessive emission of carbon dioxide into the earth's atmosphere, thus creating a kind of blanket which prevents the escape of heat generated by the sun's ultraviolet rays. As the earth's temperatures increase, and there are indications that this increase may amount to two to three degrees centigrade by the year 2050, agricultural practices in the temperate zones are disrupted by altered weather patterns. At the poles the ice caps melt, causing the seas to rise, and coastal lands, including some of the earth's major cities, become uninhabitable. Though this does indeed sound like a science fiction scenario, reputable scientists, including those involved in the *Global 2000* study, believe it to be quite possible. But we may not know for certain the calamitous results of humanity's pollution of the air until too late—if, that is, we wait until the definitive scientific data have been collected and the consequences have already begun to make themselves felt.

Our discussion of strains upon the biosystem has brought us from soil erosion to the possibility of melting ice caps, and much that might have been said about threats to our natural environment has of necessity been omitted. Yet one thing will have been obvious as a *leitmotif* appearing repeatedly in these observations: nothing in creation exists in isolation from all else. Everything in nature is interrelated in a marvelously delicate balance, and damage to one area of the whole is likely to produce consequences in another.

Today *every* part of the biosystem, nature in its totality, is under attack simultaneously: the land, the seas, the air, the forests, underground water tables, even the earth's steady temperatures.

For Christians everywhere, but perhaps especially for wealthy North American Christians, the question which presents itself with compelling force is this: can we any longer pretend that our high-waste, high-consumption style of life is defensible? Can we continue to suppose that it is compatible with the imperatives which human survival urges upon us? Can we any longer believe that in any measure it conforms to our responsibility as stewards of the earth entrusted to us by a God whom we worship as Creator and Sustainer? If we cannot, then the Christian community in America faces a massive restructuring of its value system, examining piece by piece every phase of contemporary life: from transportation systems to eating habits, from home construction to city planning, from land use to our participation in a political and economic system which apparently cannot or will not take seriously the possibility that *quality of life*—not the sheer number of material objects produced, used, then cast aside—might be a reasonable measure of our success as a society.

At this juncture, the Bible becomes a vital resource for contemporary Christians seeking to live responsibly in a global village where scarcity will increasingly be the watchword and where threats to a sustainable earth have already come dangerously close to the point at which irreversible trends are set in motion. The doctrine of creation, long neglected in American Christian thought, sheds light on our situation. The authors of Genesis, it will be recalled, state that God created the heavens and the earth, the seas and rivers, the plants and animals and fishes, as well as man and woman, in six days. After each day's labor, God looked at his handiwork and declared it "good." On the sixth day after the job was done and he could survey the whole of his creation, God pronounced it to be "very good."

Having made man and woman, God appointed them to oversee the creation. In some translations God gives humanity "dominion" over the animals and plants, but this word suggests more independence and more rights of exploitation than the original Hebrew word was intended to convey. Man and woman are trustees of the earth, stewards who hold the earth in a form of partnership with God but who are always responsible to him for the use they make of their trusteeship.

Later, as documented in the Exodus stories and the Deuteronomic codes, God rescues his chosen people out of bondage, gives them a good and fertile land and establishes them as a *community*, a community with a special understanding of itself as answerable to Yahweh, the Lord of Creation, who has graciously called the community into being. There is a certain parallelism here which should not be missed: as "man" and "woman" were created out of clay and given to each other in a relationship which images the concept of community itself and were called to be the stewards of the earth, so the Israelites were brought to the Promised Land where they were to establish a new life based on priniciples of equity, justice, and caring which make true community possible. They too were charged with responsibility for the land's condition—letting it lie fallow periodically, and tending it with that faithful attention which makes it a heritage worth passing on to future generations. Creation and community are biblical themes which I believe American Christians would do well to repossess as they attempt to understand and respond to the challenges of the present state of the earth. When seen from the biblical perspective which the creation story provides, humanity's relationship to the earth precludes the kind of voracious devouring of its substance that our dominant American lifestyle necessitates. Faithfulness to the Lord of Creation requires honoring his work in all of its manifestations, and violation of the earth is no lesser sin than murder or adultery.

Once it is recognized that nature is not something separate from and alien to humanity, to be subdued and "conquered," but rather something to be nurtured, then the relevance of the biblical doctrine of community to our contemporary situation becomes evident. For community is possible only where individuals have respect for each other and for the space they inhabit together. It is possible to meet the needs of everyone in the community only when there is a sense of "right sharing," of providing from what is ultimately the Lord's, not the property of any individuals except insofar as they hold it in trusteeship. Community is possible only when those who participate in it recognize the folly of each appropriating as much as he can of what is available, of what has been given as an extension of the creation itself for the blessing of all.

Community is possible only when men and women acknowledge that what has been provided for humankind's sustenance is sufficient (if carefully used and equitably distributed), but not limitless. Each member of the community must consider conscientiously what his or her genuine needs may be, in order that, in fulfilling these, the needs of other members of the community not be left unattended. Community, finally, is possible only when those who belong to the community feel a deep-seated love of the material resources which make possible community, and even life itself: the land, the forests, the rivers and seas, the air, the sunshine. In a genuine community, I suspect, those who feel profoundly wedded to that community spend considerable time in ritual and ceremony, celebrating their participation in the group and affirming, as did Yahweh when he rested from his labors on the eve of that first Sabbath, that his work was and is "very good."

While I do not believe in easy panaceas for the ills of a nation, I suspect that much of the social and spiritual malaise, the psychological disorientation, the disintegration of family life, the increase of crimes of all sorts afflicting this society can be attributed to the collapse of real community in our time. This, of course, is hardly a novel idea. I merely wish to stress that a recovery of community (something already taking place in urban self-reliance projects, in rural communes, in "intentional communities" within and without the institutional church) may be necessary for our continuation as a coherent social and political entity and indeed for our very survival.

But ultimately, what is even more important and more difficult is that we come to understand that the community to which we must give final allegiance is the community of the human family. Nothing less will do if we wish to be faithful to the teachings of him whom we call Lord and who again and again forces us to ignore barriers of class and race and nationality. And nothing less is required if we wish to be faithful collaborators with that Creator God who desires for his children life, not death. Life on a planet nurtured, and tended, and lovingly cared for by persons dedicated to sustaining and passing on to future generations a work of divine artistry which all can experience as being "very good."

Such an understanding of our place in the total human community would necessitate a radical reexamination of our values and a concomitant alteration in our individual and corporate lifestyles. What the lifestyle of any one of us would finally look like would no doubt be determined by many factors. But surely one common ingredient in the quest for a responsible Christian lifestyle would be greater simplicity—in housing and furnishings, in clothing, in automobiles, in entertaining, in Christmas giving, in accommodations when traveling. The list could be expanded almost endlessly.

And surely our lifestyles would signal our membership in a company of persons determined to resist the pressures of contemporary American society toward the accumulation of things. We might also discover the joy of living in greater harmony with the earth, with our fellow humans, and with ourselves as we turn city and suburban lawns into vegetable gardens, cooperate with neighbors in establishing a community cannery, engage in cooperative self-reliance projects utilizing solar energy devices or electricity-generating windmills on city apartment buildings, or help establish a club or church group where simplified, self-reliant living could be taught and shared.

If American churches, as institutions, took seriously the multiple crises associated with the rapid deterioration of the physical bases of life and began to ask really radical questions about *their* corporate lifestyles—in the light of the life and teachings of Jesus the Christ, then a revolution in American Christianity of incalculable significance would be a virtual inevitability. That revolution could well lead to a revitalization of the Church in this country and to the turning of Christians from an oftentimes narcissistic preoccupation with narrowly parochial matters to a concern for the life of the world. And we Christians might then become the leaven of the loaf that we are called to be.

Whatever lifestyle we wealthy American Christians choose, however, one thing is certain: our present style of life is possible for only a tiny fraction of the earth's inhabitants and is possible for that fraction only for a limited period of time. If we do not voluntarily impose restraints upon our appetites, nature herself will teach us limits. Already she is doing so everywhere on the planet. We have only to look and listen to discover that the web of being resembles a beautiful, intricately woven fabric. Properly cared for, it can be passed on from generation to generation, but once torn, the unraveling becomes irreversible.

For Response and Reflection

• E.F. Schumacher wrote in *Small Is Beautiful* "every increase of needs tends to increase our dependence on outside forces over which one cannot have control . . . ." Here is a simple way to test the truth of this statement. Go look in your refrigerator and kitchen cupboards. What percentage of the food you depend on for survival was (1) homegrown? (2) grown in your county? (3) produced by companies with corporate headquarters outside your state?

• Invite your county extension agent or a representative of the planning commission for your region to speak to a church group about loss of agricultural land in your area or about the future of the regional water supply.

• Another interesting check on the extent of dependence built into our lives is to research the flow of money in a community. A regional planning office, some banks, or a reference librarian can help you discover how much of the money earned in your city or county stays in the local community.

• Spend time studying in depth chapter 26 of Deuteronomy. What support do you find for the allegiance to the total human family urged by this chapter's author?

Chapter 7

Responsible Technology, Responsible Living

by David Crean

All our knowledge brings us nearer to our ignorance,
All our ignorance brings us nearer to death,
But nearness to death no nearer to God.[1]

Our technology is our pride and joy. Our technology gives us warmth, light, automobiles, dishwashers, digital watches, calculators, space probes, and a myriad of devices that render life more comfortable, more pleasant, and, above all, more convenient.

The flick of a switch gives us instant, convenient entertainment to the detriment of orchestras and theatre companies which have to exist on larger and larger subsidies and more and more expensive admission prices. We step into a convenient automobile to drive five, fifty, five hundred, or five thousand miles and forget about the decaying public transportation systems in our cities. Our supermarkets give us a plenitude of conveniently packaged and presented foods so that we can forget that anything as mundane as a cow produced a carton of milk.

Where is the life we have lost in living?
Where is the wisdom we have lost in knowledge?
Where is the knowledge we have lost in information?[2]

We are persuaded that the goods spawned by technology will bring happiness. A cursory examination of newspaper advertising, glossy magazines, and television can show this.

Face cream will banish nerves, floor wax will bring in neighbors for a cheery bridge game or gossip, grandchildren

49

will love you if your disposition improves with the right
laxative, storekeepers and pharmacists overflow with sound
avuncular advice, the right beer endows you with hearty
masculine identity, and almost anything from deodorants to
cigarettes, toothpaste, hair shampoos, and lately even antacids
will bring on love-affairs, usually on horseback or on a beach.[3]

Social critics have pointed up the underlying fallacy. The photo-
graphs of Robert Frank disclose the hollowness behind this assumption. His "Picnickers on Belle Isle, Detroit, 1955" in particular
shows empty, miserable people in an otherwise pleasurable setting.
In another photograph, "Fourth of July, Joy, New York, 1955,"
nobody is smiling.

Moreover, the sacrifices demanded by our technology are becoming excessive.

> In order to build a road, we destroy several thousand acres of
> farmland forever, all in perfect optimism, without regret,
> believing that we have gained much and lost nothing. In order
> to build a dam, which like all human things will be temporary,
> we destroy a virgin stream forever, believing that we have
> conquered nature and added significantly to our stature. In
> order to burn cheap coal, we destroy a mountain forever,
> believing, in the way of lovers of progress, that what is of
> immediate advantage to us must be a permanent benefit to the
> universe.[4]

To understand this Gadarene rush to more and better technology,
we must understand the perennial pursuit of happiness. To understand technology we must understand energy.

The early hunter-gatherer, in his pursuit of food consumed about
three thousand calories of energy per day. The advent of fire raised
this to eight thousand. The use of draft animals to twelve thousand.
By the advent of the Christian era, the annual consumption of coal
equivalent per person had reached some 1300 pounds, and the
population of the world (then some 250 million) was consuming the
equivalent of 150 million tons of coal annually. In 1970, the world
was consuming the equivalent of seven billion tons of coal. In
America, the energy consumption per person was the equivalent of
eleven tons of coal annually. Breaking down the figures, the 950

million inhabitants of the rich world consumed 5,700 million metric tons of coal equivalent; the 2,440 million poor consumed about 720 million metric tons.[5] The consequences of this ever increasing profligate use of energy are discussed in several notable books, especially in chapter 9 of Barry Commoner's *The Closing Circle*.[6] All this is not to say that technology is futile. Mankind has used technology for centuries to circumvent limits—economic limits as well as population limits. "Applying technology to the natural pressures that the environment exerts against any growth process has been so successful in the past that a whole culture has evolved around the principle of fighting against limits rather than learning to live with them."[7] The authors of *Limits to Growth* have posed the question whether it is better to live within limits or to seek ways of circumventing them until a new limit arises.[8]

> Whether 'tis nobler in the mind to suffer
> The slings and arrows of outrageous fortune
> Or to take arms against a sea of troubles,
> And by opposing end them?[9]

The illustration used is that of the whaling industry which, as larger species such as the blue whale have been killed off, has moved to smaller species. More and more whales are killed by bigger and more powerful boats. However, less and less whale oil has been produced, and the efficiency of the industry has dropped precipitously.[10] There are all too many indications today that our use of technology to bypass limits has finally reached its limit. Technology has finally created its own limits. This is difficult to grasp. After all, we have used the old approach so successfully for so many years that it seems inconceivable that it no longer works and that we must seek an alternative. There is, of course, a grave danger here. We tend to polarize our arguments into an either/or situation. Either more and better technology to overcome the limits or a slide back into an apocalyptic depression. Hazel Henderson states the dilemma as follows:

> We must avoid the dual traps of escapism or becoming destructively apocalyptic. Today's escapists are dreaming of

pristine new paradises in space, where . . . the "high frontier" of space colonies can accommodate our expansionism and competitive spirit . . . The other trap is that of the apocalypse. In our frustration, there is a tendency . . . almost to welcome the awful catharsis of apocalypse—where the Gordian knot is cut with a swift blow and the deck is swept clean, as by the mighty, cleansing tidal wave.[11]

It seems to me that these choices are not mutually exclusive. We don't have to choose either the escapism of high technology or the apocalypse. There are all too many who wish to present this apparent choice to us. These "choices" are points on a continuum, or a spectrum, if you like. It is like being told that you can have either red or blue and not being told that there are such colors as orange, yellow, and green and other intermediate shades.

Of course we need technology. But what sort? It strikes me that we need intermediate technologies, appropriate technologies, technologies with a human face, technologies that seek to conform to the limits rather than to overcome the limits. "We already live on a spaceship more wondrous than we know, and our present task, it seems to me, is first to tune in to its operating principles, which are peacefulness, humility, honesty, cooperation, and love."[12]

There is much confusion about the terms "appropriate" and "intermediate" technology. Both are taken to imply an inferior type of technology—a cheap technology. This is the trap to which many Third World nations have succumbed. The consciousness appears to be growing that the chimera of industrialization is just that. It all depends upon what you mean by "inferior." Inferior to what? Is a traditional wrist watch inferior to a digital? Is an abacus inferior to a pocket digital calculator? Is a painting inferior to a photograph? A paintbrush to a camera? A sailboat to a powerboat? The easiest way to define appropriate, intermediate, or soft technologies is to describe what they look like. They:

> are ecologically sound
> require small energy inputs
> have low or no pollution rates
> have low specialization requirements and are
> easily understandable

are compatible with local cultures
are labor intensive.

There are other distinctions, but these will do for now.[13]

Two other distinctions are important for our consideration. First, these technologies provide jobs which are psychologically rewarding, and second, there is little distinction between work and leisure.

This is where the tie-in with lifestyle occurs. To many of us, work time and leisure time are compartmentalized. Work is what we do to earn leisure. Leisure is the time that we spend in being creative and in recreating our being.

The problem with leisure is that we have compartmentalized it. We have split it off from other activities. Work forms one component. Leisure another. Religion yet another. All too often do we fail to make the connection between these. All too often do we fail to integrate our life activities. We are like many students who fail to see the connection between the many subjects which they learn. Chemistry 101 is put into a compartment with that label, and the relationship and relevance of that subject to a course in biology is seldom explored.

One of the myths of technology is that it frees us from the drudgery of work: it allows the perfectibility of humanity; the blossoming of creativity. This does not appear to have occurred to any significant degree.

If technology had generously liberated us from work, if we were genuinely able to pursue perfectibility, would we have all the ills that appear to afflict our society? Would crime be escalating? Would the rates for alcoholism, divorce, child abuse be pursuing an upward climb? Would unemployment be so high?

Our technologies would appear to have brought us material goods, but not the psychological skills to enjoy them. They have brought us convenience, but not the ability to relate to our fellow human beings.

Our vaunted technology is born of the materialism that seems, paradoxically, to have emerged from the Age of Reason. The Newtonian world system showed that God and his holy angels were not necessary to the observed motions of the stars and planets. The great French mathematician, Laplace, was able to reply with perfect equanimity when asked by Napoleon why God was not mentioned in his *Mécanique Céleste* "I never had any need of that hypothesis." [14] God was not in His Heaven, and yet all was well with the world. The Greek divorce between matter and spirit was now essentially complete despite the warnings of Jesus; St. John stresses that in his first letter.

The Godless god of technology finally held sway. Its sacrifices were human dignity and spirituality. Its apotheosis in the final analysis was the mushroom cloud over Hiroshima; the gas ovens of Auschwitz; and the mechanical horrors of Verdun, the Somme, and Ypres in the First World War. "The rift between soul and body, the Creator and the creation, has admitted the entrance into the world of the machinery of the world's doom." [15]

We must ask ourselves, therefore, what would an integrated life absolved of materialism look like. What would be the type of life where work, leisure, and our spiritual being would be totally integrated? This is an especially valid question to ask in an age when the mechanistic Newtonian physics has been superceded by the relativistic Einsteinian.

I have already suggested that the technologies that would be spawned by this would differ significantly from those that exist today. Henry David Thoreau probably said it as well as anyone when he observed: "Shall we forever resign the pleasure of construction to the carpenter? When is this division of labor to end and what object does it finally serve?" It is more than likely that such a lifestyle would not be individual. The Gospel of Jesus Christ admits not of rugged individualism but of individuals acting in concert, in community. The lifestyle would thus be communal with a sharing of values and of tasks, and yet diversity would be welcomed. Division of labor would be minimal. Within larger communities, such as cities, the concept of the neighborhood would become central. The community would not become exclusive, which is itself a temptation, but would not be too inclusive. Family living would be a blend of the nuclear family and the extended. These are also not mutually exclusive.

It is not too far from the mark to say that the community of disciples surrounding Jesus encompassed some of these principles. As far as diversity is concerned, a community containing both an arch-patriot, such as Simon the Zealot, and a collaborator of the occupying army, like Matthew the tax-collector, is about as diverse as may be wished. It would be instructive to go through a Gospel and look at how Jesus acted out his lifestyle. The life of the early church as described in the Acts of the Apostles (2:42–47; 4:32–35) and the congregation of Thessalonians addressed by Paul in two letters bear some of the hallmarks. Paul himself lived out many of these precepts (I Thessalonians 1:9).

This is not to say that products of our technology are harmful. Far from it. The automobile may be a blessing. We have allowed it to become a curse. The computer may be of great value. Cameras, stereos, television sets, tape recorders have enormous utility. When, however, they become more than the tools and toys that they are; when they (or their acquisition) become an end rather than a means; when they are set up as gods, then we reap the consequence of our own actions.

For Response and Reflection

• Leaf through a magazine that includes advertising. Try to state the values or assumptions which underlie each advertisement. What reward for buying the product is promised or hinted at by the ad? Which ones do you want to believe? Why?

• Discuss the statement by the author: "Our technologies would appear to have brought us material goods, but not the psychological skills to enjoy them. They have brought us convenience, but not the ability to relate to our fellow human beings."

• Take time to increase your awareness of alternative, intermediate technology by using one of the resources recommended at the end of the chapter. Or invite someone to talk to your group about personal experience in the field (for example, use of wind or solar energy, food cooperatives, community garden).

• Imagine a spectrum of attitudes toward technology and the world. At one end is "Go-getter Gertrude," who advocates grabbing all the gusto today and assumes new technology will solve any problems created by present technology. At the other end is "Spaceship Sally," who feels that technology is appropriate only if it expresses and enables principles like cooperation, honesty, love, humility, and peacefulness. Would you be nearer Gertrude or Sally in the spectrum? Discuss this question with others.

Chapter 8

Responses to Change

Goodbye More—Hello Less
by David Dodson-Gray

Public Anger
We Americans have witnessed strong and sometimes alarming expressions of public anger in various local situations in recent years. Limited growth increases such anger, and I expect that both organized and disorganized expressions of such anger will increase. Church professionals need to assess this public mood and discover what implications limited growth suggests for pastoral ministry.

The 1970s were a decade for shock, a time during which we denied and turned away from the basic changes that had already taken place in our fundamental situation. We "lived with" the symptoms—"stagflation," declining productivity, a deep recession (or depression), the energy crisis, stubbornly high levels of unemployment, recurrent bouts of double-digit inflation—but we denied that these are anything but temporary difficulties which will go away with good management or better leaders. The public, and the experts, did not want to believe that the end of an era was at hand.

Then came anger.

What are we to make of this sequence?

Slowing growth involves emotions of loss and impotence—impotence because we feel powerless to prevent the loss from taking place. We might find parallels between public morale now and what Doctor Elizabeth Kübler-Ross, in her recent book, *On Death and Dying*, observed in individuals who were coping with loss of loved ones or with loss of their own lives. We in the United States in the 1970s were a people beginning to go through a similar process as we experienced the loss of our earlier rates of economic growth and all of the cultural values that growth provided.

Growth has provided us reassuring milestones by which to measure progress. The American Dream itself was often perceived in terms of economic growth. Growth delayed our having to come to terms with inequality and injustice. Growth also provided a talisman of hope in tomorrow. So long as we could grow, we could believe that everyone would soon be better off.

The loss of growth brings into question that sort of hope for a better tomorrow. As growth slows, and in many areas decline is perceived, a shared dream is dying. All of us are grieving over what this means for us and for other as the benefits of a brighter economic future slip beyond our reach.

The Stages of Coping with Loss

There is a distinctive constellation of emotional and behavioral crises involved in coping with loss as Kübler-Ross pointed out in her pioneering work. She and her colleagues identified five coping mechanisms: denial, anger, bargaining, depression, and finally, acceptance. Each coping mechanism dominates at one stage in the grieving process and gives that state its name, then later subsides in intensity. But the emotion or behavior does not disappear once it has subsided. It may be momentarily re-evoked at any time. *Denial* functions as a buffer. We are shocked by the severe and unexpected turn of events in the energy crisis. Our society depends upon energy and the source of much of the energy we need is no longer controlled by us. We act as if we were numbed. It is characteristic of denial that we compartmentalize our thinking so that we ignore for more or less extended periods of time the truth we cannot yet face. How many people have you heard flatly declare: "There is no energy shortage!" We clothe ourselves in denial while we absorb the situation and collect ourselves. Denial gives way to *anger*. "Why me? Why now?" And resentment and envy accompany anger in the transition to less growth.

Anger is easily displaced and directed at others. We blame oil companies and cartels and leadership. Indeed, they are profiting from our predicament, but that predicament of limited energy remains.

Envy and resentment accompany anger, and *guilt* over our own contribution to the predicament. Anger over blame and anger at our own powerlessness are important dimensions. Our anger is reaching out for the potency and control which are being lost.

Denial and anger often alternate or even exist side by side. They are necessary and important stages, but they express the pain of loss rather than any beginning to come to grips with the emerging new reality.

Bargaining is the important first step toward coming to grips with the difficult new reality of limited growth. Bargaining is essentially an effort to postpone. We set self-imposed deadlines. We seek rewards for good behavior such as shutting off lights, turning down the heat, driving slowly. We try to compensate for our past profligacy with energy. By bargaining, we try to evade or postpone coming to grips with a world which has ceased to grow for us. But still we are not rewarded. Prices continue to rise. The only thing there is "more" of is inflation.

Depression comes when we realize that no evading or postponing will work. In our gut we realize there is a process underway involving a fundamental change through which we must go. Our depression is partly reactive—we grieve past opportunities now gone forever. "Why didn't I take a risk and buy that—three years ago when it was so comparatively cheap?" Guilt is again a factor, but it can be overcome by making amends, by doing what still can be done with the opportunities which remain. The larger part of the depression is our sadness over impending losses. It has a preparatory character and is accompanied by expressions of anticipatory fears and fantasies. This sadness is not helped by reassurances or encouragement, but by a heightened sense of being-with, belonging, solidarity.

Feelings matter most now, not words. Others may still want to continue bargaining (evasion, postponement), but attempts to change destiny are not at all helpful for those in depression. They jar the saddening process of looking in the eye and letting go of what must be let go.

Finally there comes *acceptance,* a gradual separating from what has been. We detach slowly, and we need, at this stage, reassurances that we are not alone and we have not been forgotten. Politically, these reassurances are of great importance to all who were not very rich or powerful. We need a sense of our own dignity now as we begin to bind off the ways we have lived in the world that is passing from us. Our grieving has been a kind of emotional hemorrhaging, and as that stops, the immediacy of our participation with what is ending declines. Now we can let go the sense of participation and mutuality we felt in what has passed away. Now we can turn toward the new meanings which are being built, toward the participation and mutuality which lie ahead.

It is as all this emerges from us and begins to draw us toward it that our transition from a society of growth to a sustainable society will be completed.

The public's current mood of anger is its reaction to change in long-term economic trends that became apparent durings the 1970s. I suggest, and leave to the reader to confirm or deny, that such anger is only one of a constellation of emotions we can increasingly expect to see.

Facing up to What Is Passing
We have a choice in this transition. We can go through these turbulent feelings and behaviors either at their mercy, or we can understand their function. The latter alternative will make the experience no less painful, but it will help us deal with it more constructively.

Facing up to the existence of the grieving process that comes with economic stagnancy is an important first step, for it starts us assessing all that growth has meant to us. Then we can even begin to perceive what we have not lost. And as we begin to mobilize human resources and social processes to rebuild, from our grief will gradually be born a vision of a new and potentially good life, possible for us and for those who come after us.

Living with Denial
If we recognize that denial is a radical defensive measure used to buffer ourselves and institutions from severe shock, we can appreciate its function and no longer seek to destroy it.

Technology, government, and many institutions are still tuned in to continued growth rather than accommodating their constituencies to the slowing process. Any redirection to assist the transition to a slower rate of activity will first be experienced as ''betrayal'' or ''failure'' by constituents who still believe past rates of growth are possible. But rather quickly the general and total denial breaks up into selective denial of particular parts of the experience. We are never completely blind to reality, particularly painful reality. Beneath our denial there is concern about what is happening to us and what we might be doing to help ourselves.

Living with Anger

We must expect anger in ourselves, in others, and in the responses of various institutions and institutional leaders. We need to work on ways of helping one another on all levels to express our angry hemorrhaging of feelings in words rather than in physically and socially destructive violence.

It has been found, for example, that when there is a sharp increase in unemployment, there is a correspondingly sharp rise in the physical abuse of children by angry parents and wives by angry husbands. All need help in channeling angry reactions from actions into words. The anger expressed in words then needs help to become focussed so that it moves existing organizations or becomes driving forces behind new ones. Instead of anger festering and its violence poisoning our homes, city streets, and the body-politic, it can become powerful and take its place as one of the forces shaping what emerges from the transition.

Political clubs, as well as ethnic and minority churches, have long helped like-minded angry individuals to get together to organize and articulate their interests. Labor unions have also done this. But new anguish and new anger often burst old boundaries and reach beyond old ethnic and institutional definitions. Those without organizations or access to power are going to need new ways of getting their concerns built into the new America we will be building.

Compensatory Experiences of Potency

A sense of personal competence is central to the stages of bargaining, depression, and acceptance. We can live through great loss provided we feel we have the capacity to build anew effectively.

We are shifting the center of meaning in our lives away from a past which is being lost toward an unknown future. In the transition from unsustainable patterns of economic growth, our lives will have to center on satisfactions that have been secondary, or peripheral, or perhaps not even part of our experience. The various compensatory experiences we can begin to emphasize now are important to the shift. A compensatory experience of potency gives us a new sense of why life will be worth living despite loss, a new sense of how things can be done "by" rather than "to" us.

Jobs can be redesigned to be empowering experiences in which we can grow in skill, creativity, judgment, and decision-making. Sharing work so as to eliminate unemployment can begin now so as to draw the unemployed back into the mainstream of social power. This may mean that everyone must work fewer hours so that everyone can have work. That would mean beginning to place more time and greater emphasis upon such tasks as self-development, educating one's own self and one's own children, and parenting by both parents.

The transition will also demand of each of us greater self-sufficiency. More time and skill will have to go toward repairing, recycling, reusing. We may continue to buy energy and food from central sources, but prices, scarcities, and poorer quality will motivate us to work on our own heat and light from solar, bio-gas, or wind sources, and to grow our own food.

We have not thought much about going down (not up), having less (not more), going slower (not faster), aging (not growing up), being (not achieving). In the past, transition has been something individuals went through alone.

Slowing Non-essential Change

As growth slows, we will change what we have to in order to survive. If we do not, it will not change in spite of us. Recognizing that there are grief-costs to all changes, we can begin now by not changing simply for novelty's sake. Continuity is important. We should leave alone what does not absolutely have to change.

Preserving Societal Cohesion and Morale

With slowing growth, each of us comes to feel personally threatened. We become more concerned about our own survival and the survival of our immediate family. In the church particularly, we must work on preserving the larger cultural matrix in which we have been shaped and upon which our well-being so largely depends.

We live amid a complex and largely unacknowledged network of relationships whose coordination and smooth functioning is the indispensable presupposition of life as we have known and loved it. Not only our laws, institutions, values, and goals are part of this invisible web of societal vitality, but also our words, syntax, and sense of clarity about life's meaning and purpose.

Personal survival, as growth slows, will depend upon continued access to sufficient food, energy, and physical resources. Just as there is little point in wresting these from the earth if in the process we destroy the soil, the atmoshere, or some part of the biosphere, so, too, there is little point to strategies for personal survival which destroy our cultural matrix.

Personal survival worth the living will depend on preserving our societal support systems, for they are as vital as oxygen or water.

Institutions which embody values, dreams, goals, and symbols enable large numbers of individuals to make sustained and coordinated efforts to achieve reasonably efficient allocation of resources. Unless these societal life support systems remain relatively intact, we will witness a cultural collapse more drastic than any slowing or ending of economic growth.

The Importance of Morale and Hope

In the transition, what is central is what happens to the morale of individuals, of institutions, and of our culture as a whole. Kübler-Ross writes of the importance of respecting and preserving "a thread of hope" throughout the grieving process. We need hope to find our way out of the maze, to pull ourselves through difficult tunnel-like transitions. We need hope to sustain us until we can again more clearly see our meaning and our way.

The Church, as community and symbol of continuity, must foster this hope and provide support for coping with loss. Our goals and values matter even more now as we begin to think the heretofore unthinkable—about life after growth.

For Response and Reflection

• This chapter describes a process of responding to major changes in life and society. Does this description match your own experience? Spend some time thinking about a specific occasion in your life when you had to let go of something or someone very important to you. Some examples would include: moving to a new place; a job ending; a friendship terminated; the youngest child starting school or leaving home; a lifelong dream abandoned; the death of a loved one. Can you identify in your working through this experience the stages named by the author? What supported you in moving through denial toward acceptance?

• Discuss with others the feeling related to the present time of slower economic growth. Can you fit these feelings of yours and others into the denial-acceptance continuum outlined in this chapter? Will some people share how they were able to work through the painful stages of the process of coping with change and loss?

• Reread the last paragraph of the chapter. Can you identify ways the Church is already doing this? Can you imagine new ways for the Church to help people shape goals and values suited to a hopeful entry into "life after growth"?

• Ask a mental health professional to talk to a church group about domestic violence in your community in times of economic slowdown or increased unemployment. Discuss how the churches can help channel legitimate anger away from physical violence.

• Discuss: How does the biblical story of God and humanity give us hope as we move into a future with many demands for change?

SECTION THREE

BIBLICAL REFLECTION:

Transformation in Community
by Gary T. Evans

> I appeal to you therefore, brethren, to present your bodies as a living sacrifice, holy and acceptable to God, which is your sprirtual worship. Do not be conformed to this world but be transformed by the renewal of your mind, that you may prove what is the will of God, what is good and acceptable and perfect.
>
> *Romans 12:1–2*

Anyone who has marveled at the fragile beauty of a butterfly and pondered the amazing difference between it and the caterpillar from which it emerged is well on the way to understanding the sort of transformation urged in these verses. Metamorphosis is the English word nearest in meaning to the Greek word translated here as transformed and it means change in the essential being or character of something. Scrooge, in Dickens' *A Christmas Carol,* is a perfect example of human metamorphosis since he undergoes a transformation of his inmost self from miserly crank to joyous sharer of life and wealth.

Such a fundamental alteration is contrasted here with the state of being "conformed to this world," which means being concerned primarily with outward form and allowing one's behavior and values to match the cultural norm. The ability to see the world from God's point of view requires a "renewal of your mind," by which is meant a radically new set of values which conform more nearly to the "good and acceptable and perfect" as viewed from the divine perspective.

65

Evidence of inner transformation is identified in the first verse as the willingness and ability "to present your bodies as a living sacrifice, holy and acceptable to God..." The implied assumption is that every activity, relationship, and social structure in which bodies participate is to be seen as something done in cooperation with God. In contrast to the dead animal bodies which were offered in ceremonial sacrifices, all human acts and organizations in which the readers shared should constitute their thankful offering of life to God.

The startling assertion made in the twelfth chapter of Romans is that spiritual worship consists not of pious observances in church, but of every moment and action of daily living conformed to the will of God. One of the ancient meanings of the Greek word translated into English as worship is "that to which a person devotes life." This is very close to the meaning of worship in these verses.

Make a list of signs of conformity to this world you see in a community of which you are a part (work place, church, family, etc.). Then make a list of evidences of transformation to the will of God in the same community.

Chapter 9

Learning to Live More with Less

by Charlotte Fardelmann

Doris Janzen Longacre is known by many as the author of two books on responsible lifestyle in a world of hunger and limited resources: *More-with-Less Cookbook* (1976) and *Living More with Less* (1980), both published by Herald Press, Scottdale, Pennsylvania 15683. The second book was written under the stress of terminal cancer which ended Doris's earthly life at age thirty-nine on 10 November 1979. Her husband, Paul, who is on the staff of the Mennonite Central Committee, and others brought the book to publication.

Paul Longacre stooped to pick up a loaf of freshly-baked homemade bread and a jar of granola on his back doorstep as he greeted me at his home in Akron, Pennsylvania. "A friend in our church started making bread for us when Doris first developed cancer," he said. Now the friend makes it for Paul and the two Longacre daughters, Cara Sue, fourteen, and Marta Joy, twelve.

The bearded man quietly invited me into his kitchen, which had an air of old-fashioned simplicity, and showed me to a chair at the sturdy wooden table near the woodstove. Around the corner was an upright piano and violin, on the bookshelf a dog-eared copy of the *Holy Bible, Diet for a Small Planet, Field Guide to the Wild Flowers, Keeping Your Personal Journal,* and *Getting Well Again.*

"We both grew up on farms," said Paul. He told me Doris had suffered from asthma since the age of five, so much so, that her parents moved to Arizona for ten years to help her breathe. Strongly religious, the couple served twice under the Mennonite overseas program, 1964–1972 in Indonesia. The latter service was cut short by a nearly fatal asthma attack Doris had.

Glancing at a photograph of Doris, a tall, gentle-looking woman with a round face and peaceful eyes, I felt as if I knew her already from her books.

In the Foreword of *Living More with Less,* she talks about how hard it is to make small decisions when you stop to think what causes what.

> Oh, not enough flour! I've got to take the car and run to the store. No, I'll walk . . . I need the exercise . . . it's only a mile. But I need the flour now. The bread must start rising or it won't be done in time. Look, why am I always in a hurry? I've got to slow down, take more time to think, see the clouds, listen to Ann . . . and walking saves gasoline, energy. Everybody jumping into a car for simple errands is one reason we get that statistic . . . what is it . . . six percent of the world's population uses forty per cent of the resources. That way of living makes other people poor.
>
> But the flour. I need it. Now if the bike were here . . . but Bill took it to work. The flour! If my neighbor were home, I could borrow it . . . but she never has whole grain flour. We want to eat more whole grains . . . I've got to take the car. No way out.
>
> Wait. I don't have to make bread today. That can wait until I shop for the week . . . there's enough flour here for that good muffin recipe. And, lucky me . . . I don't have to start that until five o'clock. Ann and I can take a walk.[1]

Doris points out that responsible living is not a once-in-a-lifetime decision to throw over a comfortable way of life for stark monastic ways. Rather it is a series of small experiments, a path of adventure in which one step leads you on to another and in which no one ever reaches perfection.

In the beginning of the *More-with-Less Cookbook,* Doris says: "Cutting back sounds like a dismal prospect.[1] 'Let's splurge, just this once,' appeals more to North American ears. Put dismal thoughts aside then, because this book is not about cutting back. This book is about living joyfully, richly, and creatively. There is a way, I discovered, of wasting less, eating less, and spending less which gives not less, but more. The gain is so great that the phrase 'cutting back' doesn't fit at all."[2]

Paul Longacre explained how the more-with-less concept came about. The world hunger crisis in the early 1970s concerned

Christians of all faiths, and many churches set up hunger commissions at that time. The Mennonite Central Committee asked every Mennonite household to try and cut down on eating and spending by ten percent. He quoted his wife, in *Living More with Less*, "Intricate reasoning on the causes and solutions of world hunger has its place. But there are times when the only answer is 'because they have little, I try to take less.'"

The building blocks for both books are the contributions sent in by Mennonites around the world as a result of trying to follow this request to cut down by ten percent.

Along with the expected suggestions of using less beef and sugar, less processed and over-packaged food, more public transportation and solar homes, there are many ideas on how to live spiritually-richer lives.

Time is another item covered under more-with-less living, and Doris Lonacre does not believe in the phrase "time is money." She quotes Kosuke Koyama, an Asian theologian, describing time in Asia as "unlimited as a loving mother's milk to her baby." Koyama describes God as the one who "went so slow that he became nailed down in his search for man."

Doris Longacre had her own reasons for using time wisely, because, for her, time was running out.

In a sermon to her Akron Mennonite Church in April of 1978, Doris described learning you have cancer as imagining you are in darkness. "We were like people in a very dark place not knowing which way to go." She and Paul were both in graduate school at the time and had two young daughters. Recalled Doris, "Actually, we ended up going to two schools. One of these was Kansas State University. The other was a school with a much more difficult curriculum—the school for finding God's presence in the experience of having cancer."

She spoke of finding the light of God's presence, sometimes in being alone, other times in being with loved ones. "There are times when each of us has to face ourselves and face the problems that come to us in silence and aloneness. I found that deep inside of me there was a place that had to be nurtured in silence, in prayer, and in reading and studying the Bible."

Doris spoke of being aware of her "innermost" and the fact that "it needs the light of his presence, otherwise the aloneness inside of me turns into loneliness."

"When life goes easily and well, I can jog along without giving this place inside of me the attention that it needs. When things don't go well, my 'innermost' cries out for help. It cries for a healing light."

The Longacres derived much comfort and spiritual sustenance from their house church group which meets every other week. This group, plus members of the Longacre family, held a special prayer service for healing Doris. She spoke of it in her sermon. "That was an experience that we will never forget. We felt that we had lifted up the problem to God, looked at it, named it, admitted that it was there, and asked God to act. I had a strong sense of God answering our prayer. Not with a 'Yes, I will heal you' or 'No, it's not my will to heal you,' but with the words, 'I am with you.'"

Doris worked mornings at the office on *Living More with Less*. Paul remarked that she never brought one page of the book home with her. Afternoons and evenings were for family, friends, devotions, and long walks in the countryside. The book was close to completion when Doris died on November 10, 1979.

Paul said the unfinished manuscript symbolizes the fact that the task of living responsibly is never finished. He sees the fact that others had to bring this book to completion as symbolizing that no one person is a final expert on the subject. We need help from each other, and the work of many people made the completion of this book a shared effort.

As I left the Longacre home, Paul gave me a copy of Doris' own list of things life is too short for:

> Life is too short to ice cakes. Cakes are good without icing.
> Life is too short to read all the church periodicals.
> Life is too short not to write regularly to your parents.
> Life is too short to eat factory-baked bread.
> Life is too short to keep all your floors shiny.
> It's too short to let a day pass without hugging your spouse and
>   each of your children.
> Life is too short to nurse grudges and hurt feelings.
> It's too short to worry about getting ready for Christmas. Just
>   let Christmas come.

Life is too short to spend much money on neckties and earrings.

It's too short for nosy questions like, "How do you like your new pastor?" or, if there has been a death, "How's he taking it?"

It's too short to be gone from home more than a few nights a week.

It's too short not to take a nap when you need one.

It's too short to give importance to whether purses match shoes or towels match bathrooms.

It's too short to stay indoors when trees turn color in fall, when it snows, or when the spring blossoms come out.

Life is too short to miss the call to worship on a Sunday morning.

It's too short for bedspreads that are too fancy to sleep under.

Life is too short to work in a room without windows.

Life is too short to put off Bible study.

It's too short to put off improving relationships with the people that we live with.

For Response and Reflection

• What was your initial reaction to the title of this chapter? Have your feelings changed since you read the chapter?

• Can you imagine what would seem most important to you in life if you knew you only had a short time to live? What could you do *now* to emphasize what you identified as important during your imagining? Why wait?

• How does what Doris Longacre called her "innermost" get cared for in your own life? Are there adjustments in your lifestyle which would make your "innermost" less lonely in its aloneness?

• Read Doris Longacre's book, *Living More with Less*. (See Resource section.)

Chapter 10

Stepping Stones to Community
by David W. Williams

Science and theology are agreed that people are designed to live in cooperating groups. But recent decades have seen the near-disappearance of family, clan, neighborhood, tribe, and parish. In the presence of the mixed blessings of the advanced technologies of transportation, communication, and industrial production, how are we to create complementary forces which develop and preserve an element essential to human life on this planet: community?

Many people have begun developing styles of living in which their personal, social, economic, and political behaviors consciously reflect their awareness that the costs and benefits of their involvement with transportation, communication, and industry on a daily basis have to be weighed carefully in terms of preserving the human physical and social environment. Since many of the traditional patterns of community have been nearly destroyed by immigration, migration, and centralization, many of these people have formed groups to reconstruct situations which foster cooperation: intentional communities.

Some of these involve substantial commitments resulting in the establishment of a whole town. Others are more like neighborhoods, while others resemble the large families of past generations. Many are nearly invisible since they exist within what appear to be typical suburban or inner city situations and are based in social and economic relationships rather than recognizable buildings.

But how do we rediscover the skills and attitudes that make communities work in the face of so many forces which have made us competing strangers, dependent upon the monetary economy and technology? An answer is to seek the ideas and practices of community where they still exist, learn from these sources, practice these skills, and assess them and join with others for mutual support. Thus the development of a successful community, whether a residential one or that found in a circle of friends supporting lifestyle change, requires three overlapping phases of activity. *Preparation* provides for the gathering of conceptual and experiential information, the development of a shared vision of the community and occasions for the members to experience each other in a variety of roles and settings. *Assessment* offers a means of inventorying the various resources which the community will bring to its vision and a method of seeing how these resources interrelate with the community's values. *Networking* brings the community into economic, informational, and spiritual relationships with other groups where a larger scale of activity is appropriate.

It is important in preparation, as in the other stages, to be aware of our need to reintegrate many of the elements of living in community which have been separated and segregated in recent times. These themes should be carefully considered in all activities:

Interaction among generations: Are we doing things so that old and young alike are significantly involved? Are there opportunities for physical activity appropriate to everyone? Does discussion include children? Is there a relaxation of "parent-child" roles in favor of that of "community member"?

Mental/physical/spiritual integration: Do we combine productive activity and discussion? Are spiritual values related to everyday activities? Do we seek a balance among work, play, and rest?

Self-reliance and creativity: Are we confident of our natural capacity to form cooperating groups? Do we recognize that the form and style of our community will evolve out of the uniqueness of the time and place in which we find ourselves?

Packaged solutions, including curricula, technique-heavy "group-process," parliamentary and leader-oriented approaches must be resisted in favor of "home-grown" processes which reflect the unique group of individuals discovering and creating themselves.

Preparing for community is already well underway, you may be pleased to learn, since you have read this far in the book. Developing a cooperative and creative set of interrelationships in community requires more than reading up on the subject, but the experiences of others can stimulate the development and expression of the group's ideas. Planning and conducting the group's gatherings actually begins the process of living in community itself.

Books and other resources which seem to relate to the themes of the group should be surveyed and shared in an intergenerational setting which integrates discussion with productive, cooperative activity (such as preparing a meal or painting a room). Cooperative board games and activity games are another important means of experiencing community in a way which integrates concepts with experiences so that they can be shared among those of different ages and different personal styles. Gradually, more extensive community-like experiences should be undertaken, such as round robin series of weekend visits to each other's homes by three to seven members (not necessarily in family units), or a camping trip or retreat by the whole group for several days or longer. These times should seek a balance of productive and recreational; active and quiet; conceptual and experiential opportunities.

The object of preparation is to sift through the words and ideas of others to find those which strike a chord in the group, then to begin transforming these concepts into the actions, thoughts, and feelings of the group members. At the same time, these events become a way of practising or simulating community experiences, which then suggest directions for further exploration. As these experiences and bits of information accumulate, some stocktaking is a good idea. A great deal of experience informs us that taking a step back from what we are doing to get a better look at it is sometimes a problem. A framework through which to view our activities helps us to gain that perspective and to unify the perceptions of individual community members.

Such a framework which a number of communities have found helpful is presented here. (Please note that it is NOT a technique— only the community can create a particular way of using it that meets its needs and fits its styles.) We often need to remind ourselves that community exists on a number of levels, sometimes referred to as "mental/spiritual-physical." If an end is to be achieved, circumstances on these levels have to be in harmony with each other. We'll look at the framework itself and then at a few examples of how it has been used by communities to plan and deal with problems and concerns.

First we can consider six different kinds of RESOURCES or levels on which community exists:

• We live in a PLACE. This idea includes the geography, climate, etc. of the region as well as the natural features of our immediate surroundings.

• SPACES refer to the areas or enclosures which we have created or modified such as gardens, buildings, or rooms.

• OCCASIONS includes all the time-related aspects of our existence such as seasons of the year, the work week, or one's daily schedule.

• TOOLS are all those objects and machines, etc., which extend our productive/creative capacitites. (Note that this *excludes* things which restrict creativity, or things we have yet to learn how to use creatively.)

• SKILLS means all those mental/spiritual and physical capabilities which someone (or a group) has which makes it possible to deal effectively with objects and situations.

• CONCEPTS/VALUES are those shared mental/spiritual "things" such as ideas, symbols, words, beliefs, or knowledge through which we understand, organize, and evaluate all the above, yet which depend upon these physical-behavioral things for their incarnation.

These resources support functioning in four CONTEXTS:

• PRIVACY/INDIVIDUALITY refers both to being alone and to being able to act independently within the group, or to direct or lead the group in some activity. (This level is probably most critical to a community's success and the subject of the greatest concern to those who are drawn to the idea of residential community. Successful communities provide effectively for this context at all levels of resources.)

• INTIMACY means being with one (or perhaps a few) others only. (This includes relationships which are occasional and ongoing, as well as those in which sexuality is a part and those in which it is not.)

• COMMUNITY is the group as a whole. (This level is the focus, of

course, but must not overshadow the other contexts. It is also the level at which there are fewest resources available from our familiar lifestyles.)
• OUTREACH is the involvement of the community with outside groups/individuals and "the world."

These elements can be arranged to form a table like this:

INVENTORY FOR COMMUNITY

	Privacy/ Individuality	Intimacy	Community	Outreach
Places				
Spaces				
Occasions				
Tools				
Skills				
Values				

Thus the things which the community has or needs can be sorted into these boxes as a means of getting an overview and promoting productive discussion and action. For example, having individual rooms is SPACE . . . PRIVACY; speaking several languages is a SKILL . . . OUTREACH; a weekend retreat for a couple is OCCASION . . . INTIMACY; while a volleyball set is TOOL . . . COMMUNITY. As the chart is filled in, gaps or imbalances or even contradictions may appear. One community had problems with privacy which they attacked only on the value and skill levels. After inventorying, they realized that there were no individual rooms (SPACE) and no regular times for solitude (OCCASIONS). Another group responded to the needs of others to such an extent that all of their resources were concentrated under OUTREACH: this impaired COMMUNITY to a serious degree. Another set of people living in community as married couples realized, in the course of this kind of review, that special attention to the context of intimacy at all levels was needed. An inventory can be done as an exercise in the planning stages or after community formation. It can become a comprehensive planning tool or an informal "game" for sharing perceptions of the community. Such a framework can be useful in relation to a specific problem or just a periodic means of general stocktaking. Since the framework is just a means of initiating productive action, it should be *laid aside* as soon as it has provided a focus for energies.

As planning and assessment proceed, an awareness of other similar groups seeking community will develop. Planning to develop informational, spiritual, and economic relationship with other communities through networking is essential. At one point, many communities overemphasized their self-reliance to the point of isolation (COMMUNITY vs. OUTREACH) and rejected "bureaucratic" involvements at the expense of taking advantage of some pluses of larger scale economic activity.

Networking with other communities is, therefore, an essential later phase of community development. Visits to communities in the preparation stage as well as participation in workshops, celebrations, and community simulations can form the foundation for information exchange and spiritual support. Asking an experienced community member to act as a "concerned outsider" from time to time in preparation or assessment may provide needed perspective. Establishing economic relationships with other communities may involve seeking equipment or expertise with neighboring groups. An informal barter system among communities may also be considered.

Community, of course, is not a place but a way of living. Seeking it could involve very substantial changes in one's life. However, an equally effective realization of community can occur in the renewing of the cooperative relationships which already exist in one's life. Many of the most profound changes which would bring about "a community" can be brought about "right where we are" by imaginative recycling of existing resources—by rethinking the ways in which we use what we aready have.

For Response and Reflection

• Most people live in what could be called "accidental" communities, brought together by virtue of birth or occupation or marriage. The author of this chapter believes that, through a "renewing of the cooperative relationships which already exist in one's life," it is possible to develop more effective communities where we are. Make a "Table" like the one illustrated in the chapter, and use it to inventory one of the "communities" in which you participate (for example, family, church, a circle of close friends). Are there gaps or blank spots in the chart? These might point out areas in which you and others could work to strengthen such communities.

• The author emphasizes certain elements of community living which he feels are in need of greater attention today (intergenerationality; integration of the mental, physical, and spiritual; self-reliance and creativity). Discuss with others the questions he raised in regard to these elements. How are these elements being lived out in various relationships and institutions of which you are presently part?

Chapter 11

Shalom:
Toward a Vision of Human Wholeness
by Bruce C. Birch

The great polarity between power and powerlessness lies behind issues as wide-ranging as world hunger, energy use, disarmament, human rights, sexual orientation, persistent racism, disparities of wealth in and between nations, the disappearance of the family farm, and the erosion of authority in institutions.

It is proper that the Church struggle with this agenda of complex issues. Our response is usually, "What shall we do?" We generate programs, money, and strategies for action. Although action is extremely important, it becomes hollow if we do not also ask, "Who are we to be?" The Church is not simply another community action organization. We are called to act because of a perspective rooted in our identity as the people of God, the body of Christ. What we do is only as effective as the vision out of which we do it. If we are not renewing our vision, the renewal of our programs will be in vain.

For me a central question has become, "What is the vision of our own humanity in relation to God out of which we might responsibly use or even relinquish power and out of which we might hope in the midst of powerlessness?"

In answering that question and finding that vision I have been more and more drawn to the biblical symbol of *shalom*.

Most of you know *shalom* as meaning peace. Some of you may know the word as a greeting, especially in modern Israel. But the basic meaning of that Hewbrew word out of which these other uses come is wholeness. In the Old Testament *shalom* is used for that vision of wholeness that should characterize faithful life lived in relationship to God. Walter Brueggemann describes the meaning of *shalom* like this: "The central vision of world history in the Bible is that all of creation is one. Every creature in community with every other creature living in harmony and security toward the joy and well being of every other creature." *Shalom* is best understood when we experience wholeness and harmony as human beings with God, with others, and with creation itself.

The possibility of *shalom* exists by virtue of God's creation. *Shalom* is God's intention for creation. Robert McAfee Brown has suggested that for that old triangle we used to draw so often of God, Self, Others, we ought to substitute a square and put God, Self, Others, Nature. Then we come to a closer approximation of the *shalom* pointed to in creation material.

Creation Theology Themes

Three Old Testament themes point to the fullness and the richness of *shalom* as the possibility for which we were created. The first is the theme of creation in the image of God. The Bible affirms the unique and precious quality of every person as a child of God. It also affirms the responsibility of each person. To be created in the image of God is a gift that brings with it the responsibility to care for God's creation (Genesis 1:28).

The commission to have dominion over the earth is a trusteeship of divine right; a trusteeship of God's own care for the creation and an entrusting to our stewardship of that care.

A second important theme from creation theology is the goodness of creation. At the end of the sixth day, God looked at all that had been made and saw that it was *very* good (Genesis 1:31). The intention of creation was for *shalom* to be experienced by all, for all to know the goodness of creation. We in this affluent culture of ours have come to define "fullness of life" in terms of more than enough. The fuller our lives, the more excess we have beyond our basic needs. We have turned the tables on the biblical understanding. The desire of many for excess begins to deny enough for others, and the possibility of *shalom* is limited for some.

A third theme of shalom is this: in creation we are all related.

Human beings are not self-sufficient. We need relationship to God, to others, and to nature. Jesus, when asked to sum up the Law, sums it up not simply in terms of love of God but love of neighbor as well. Genesis 2:18 tells us that God saw it was not good for his human creature to be alone.The story then goes on to express relationship to nature (garden, animals) as well as with other humans. *Shalom* is the possibility of harmonious relationship with every person and with nature. We are not only created as stewards of God to experience the goodness of creation, but we are created to be in community with all creation. *Shalom* only finds its fulfillment when we find that interrelatedness.

The Distortions

Now having raised three important themes from the creation material, I want to raise two important distortions of the created possibility of *shalom*.

The first distortion is hierarchical thinking. Over the centuries in the Church the misuse of God's giving us dominion over the earth led to a hierarchical understanding which divided the relationship of the human to God and to nature. Hierarchy operated something like this: Picture a ladder of categories. At the top is God whose nature is pure spirit. At the bottom is the earth whose nature is material. You have a polarity between the spiritual and the material, the divine and the bodily. It wasn't very long before we began to make subcategories: God, then perhaps divine beings that are talked about in the Old and New Testaments, then humans, then animals, then plants, and finally the earth itself. The closer you got up the ladder to God, the higher the moral worth invested in that order of creation.

Eventually the hierarchy went: God, males, females, other races than white, Jews, then animals, plants, and the earth. Hierarchical understanding became the foundation for superstructures of sexism, racism, and anti-Semitism. If we had really understood the wholeness pictured by *shalom*, we could not have created that insidious hierarchical ladder. We would have understood that the welfare and the fullness of life for every part of creation is dependent on interrelationship and full participation.

A second distortion is the danger of defining the *shalom* of creation too narrowly. It is one thing to say that the *shalom* of creation puts us in relationship with God, others, and nature, but we have to realize how radically the Bible understood that relationship. The geography of *shalom* extends to the whole globe. We are to seek *shalom* not only in our own community, but across political and social boundaries. The scope of *shalom* extends to the nonhuman as well as to the human. *Shalom* is not simply a human property but it is that relationship of wholeness between ourselves and nature as well. The duration of *shalom* is to extend to all generations. We do not speak of *shalom* for our generation alone but for all those generations yet to come.

Structures of Shalom

I want to turn now from the possibility of *shalom* which comes to us by virtue of creation and talk about the structures of *shalom*. *Shalom* is not only the possibility for which we were created but *shalom* is the word used to describe the covenant relationship when we are truly living in community. *Shalom* is the state which existed when God's love for Israel was returned by Israel's righteousness and faithfulness. The covenant sought to embody that understanding of *shalom* in societal structures that insured the full participation in *shalom* and protected those who might be exploited or cut off from full participation and *shalom*.

One of the reasons there are so many law codes in the Old Testament, and all different, is because the job of structuring the community to express *shalom* had to be done over and over and over again—every time the social order changed. In those law codes, you find the constant concern to provide and care for those who might by some set of circumstances, intentional or unintentional, be shut off from fullness of life, shut off from the experience of *shalom*. Food and access to the legal system were regarded as basic rights which the law codes attempted to embody in the social structure. It was not enough to leave them to God or the benevolence of individuals. It was necessary to structure that concern into the community so that *shalom* was insured on the broadest possible scale.

Brokenness of Shalom

This structure of *shalom* in faithful community was made necessary by the brokenness of *shalom*, the reality of sin. We could talk at length about the biblical understanding of sin: pride, self-centeredness, disobedience.

All understandings of sin are simply ways of talking about how *shalom* gets broken. When *shalom* is broken, when wholeness is not present, when we are not experiencing harmony with God, with others, and with creation itself, then we are participating in the reality of sin. To understand sin that way is to divert us from our preoccupation with sin as moral transgression to sin as the condition of brokenness which we all experience. We are sometimes so preoccupied with individual moral concerns that we fail to see the brokenness between one another is sin in which we *all* participate.

A second point about sin in the Bible is this: If a belief in the image of God in creation means that every person is of infinite worth, a belief in sin means that no merely human structure is worthy of infinite trust. Only God is worthy of our ultimate trust. Our loyalties to nations, classes, race, groups, lifestyles are always secondary. All of these loyalties are to be submitted to the Lordship of God who alone is sovereign over creation. As Christians we must ask ourselves, do my personal loyalties serve to create unity (*shalom*) among persons or do they separate me from those who are of different races, classes, or lifestyles. If our loyalties create division, then we are seeing our own participation in sin, for to serve God's *shalom* is to work for reconciliation.

A third point about sin is that if the vision of *shalom* calls us to lead in building faithful structures of wholeness, then our knowledge of the brokenness of *shalom* calls for us to lead as well in repentance. We must seek out and confess the ways in which we too have contributed to and participated in the breaking of the wholeness and harmony for which we were created.

Restoration of Shalom

This brings me to the fourth theme concerning *shalom*. If we truly live in a broken world, as I believe we do, then the real question for us is how *shalom* gets restored. For Christians, Jesus Christ is the fulfillment and embodiment of *shalom*. In him that which was broken is made whole, that which was divided is reunited. It is appropriate that Jesus should be referred to by the title of Isaiah 9: the Prince of Peace, the Prince of *Shalom*.

In Ephesians 2 the language of *shalom* is explicitly claimed as the meaning of Jesus for the Church. Listen to this familiar passage with new ears: "But now in Christ Jesus you who once were far off have been brought near in the blood of Christ. For he is our peace." (The word standing behind this word is ultimately *shalom*. For he is our *shalom*.) "who has made us both one and has broken down the dividing wall of hostility . . . that he might create in himself one new person in place of the two, so making peace (*shalom*) and might reconcile us both to God in one body through the cross, thereby bringing the hostility to an end. And he came and preached peace (*shalom*) to those who were near." It is Christ who makes us whole in unity with our neighbor.

In this spirit of Christ's *shalom*, the Church has to ask more seriously, "Who are those far off who have been brought near?" Are they not the dispossesed as well as the privileged? Are they not the outcasts as well as the acceptable. Are they not our nonhuman neighbors as well as our human ones? The dividing walls of hostility which separate rich from poor, hungry from satisfied, powerful from powerless, humanity from the rest of nature must be broken down if the Church is to serve the Prince of *Shalom*. The pattern is Christ himself who knew no barriers to other persons. As Ephesians makes clear, Jesus made *shalom* both as incarnation, the taking flesh, and as atonement, the sacrifice on the cross.

The *shalom* of Jesus Christ is incarnational. As the Word was made flesh in Jesus Christ, we too are called upon to embody in the flesh the vision of *shalom*.

But the *shalom* of Jesus Christ is also cruciform. Thus if we are to make *shalom* as Christ has made *shalom*, it is to take up the cross. It will require becoming vulnerable to the pain of the world whenever we encounter it. It will require a willingness to die.

Wholeness through the Eucharist
One of the central ways in which the vision of Christ's *shalom* is kept before us is in the Eucharist. It is that gathering for the sacrament of communion, the Lord's Supper. No other activity of the Church so fully gathers all the elements of *shalom* and Jesus Christ than this sacramental act. The common elements of bread and wine point the Church to the concrete realities of the incarnation. They remind us of

the biblical unity of concern for life's bread and the bread of life. As the bread is broken and the wine poured, we are reminded of Christ's sacrifice, but his brokenness is also one with the brokenness of all creation. The sacramental table becomes a window on our world and does not allow us to use the moment of our partaking as a retreat. It impels us into the broken world for which Christ is broken. And when we partake of the Eucharist, we receive the brokenness of the world into ourselves, because we know that we are a part of that brokenness, and we know that with Christ we accept the pain of suffering and despair as God's servants. We make ourselves vulnerable once again to realities of our world from which we might have succeeded in isolating and insulating ourselves.

But here is the good news of the Gospel! In taking this brokenness, this pain, this suffering, into ourselves in this sacramental act, we are not consumed with sorrow but filled with Thanksgiving. How remarkable that the word for this sacramental act is Eucharist, which in Greek means Thanksgiving. In partaking of the broken bread, we are united, and made whole. Eucharist is *shalom*. Eucharist is wholeness. Crucifixion becomes resurrection. Death becomes life. Judgment becomes hope. Broken creation becomes new creation. This is the vision which moves the Church. It is not the wisdom of the world. But it is the mandate of those sent from the Eucharist table of God's people.

In terms of worldly wisdom, this is all a paradox. But in the words of I Corinthians 1:27−28, "God chose what is foolish in the world to shame the strong. God chose what is low and despised in the world, even things that are not, to bring to nothing, things that are."

Shalom stands as one of the great symbols of our biblical vision. Pointing us to the possibility of creation in us all, calling us to work for faithful community structures to embody *shalom*, confronting us with our participation in the brokenness of *shalom* and reminding us of the one in whom we are restored to wholeness. It is small wonder that when we gather as the Christian church we so often choose to close with the words of Aaron's blessing from the sixth chapter of Numbers:

> The Lord bless you and keep you:
> The Lord make his face to shine upon you,

and be gracious to you;
The Lord lift up his countenance upon you
and give you peace (*Shalom*).

For Response and Reflection

• The author of this chapter declares that the Church's actions will be hollow without a clear answer to the question, "Who are we to be?" State briefly in your own words his responses to this question as he relates it to the four aspects of *shalom* dealt with here. Several people could compare what they have written.

• Imagine a square of fabric in which green, orange, brown, and yellow threads are interwoven. Let this fabric symbolize your present life. The green thread can stand for God, orange for others, brown for nature, and yellow for yourself. Would the colors be about equal in your present experience of life, or would some be more dominant than others? Would the different colors tend to intersect or be distinct sections of the cloth? What does this imaginary colored cloth demonstrate to you about your present experience of *shalom* as wholeness and harmony of self with God, others, and nature?

• In a group, discuss this statement by the author: "Only God is worthy of our ultimate trust. Our loyalties to nations, classes, race, groups, lifestyles are always secondary." It will be useful to consider this statement as part of a careful study of the sixth chapter of Matthew, verses 25–33.

• Read the front and editorial pages of a recent issue of a newspaper. As you read, make two lists: (1) evidence of societal structures that enable full participation in *shalom* and protect those who might be exploited; and (2) evidence of societal structures and attitudes that tend to break down harmony among human beings, God, and nature. Several people who do this can compare lists.

• What is your response to this question to the American church posed by the author (in the original full-length article): "Can a church preoccupied with institutional success and burdened by material comfort go to the cross for the sake of *shalom* in a broken world?"

SECTION FOUR

BIBLICAL REFLECTION:

The World as Community

During the seven plenteous years the earth brought forth
abundantly, and he [Joseph] gathered up all the food of the
seven years when there was plenty in the land of Egypt, and
stored up food in the cities; he stored up in every city the food
from the fields around it. And Joseph stored up grain in great
abundance, like the sand of the sea, until he ceased to measure
it, for it could not be measured.

The seven years of plenty that prevailed in the land of Egypt
came to an end; and the seven years of famine began to come,
as Joseph had said. There was famine in all lands; but in all the
land of Egypt there was bread. When all the land of Egypt was
famished, the people cried to Pharaoh for bread; and Pharaoh
said to all the Egyptians, "Go to Joseph; what he says to you,
do." So when the famine had spread all over the land, Joseph
opened all the storehouses, and sold to the Egyptians, for the
famine was severe in the land of Egypt. Moreover, all the earth
came to Egypt to Joseph to buy grain, because the famine was
severe all over the earth.

Genesis 41:47–49, 53–57

Anyone who has paid attention to the crafting of a film realizes that a
close-up shot emphasizes actions or emotions the director wants to
be certain the audience sees. The same is true when a television
camera isolates a key action in order to interpret its impact on the
flow of a sporting event.

Similarly, the narrator of the forty-first chapter of Genesis
focuses the reader's attention on a small cast of characters, and in
telling their story, he invites his audience to see the entire world
through his eyes. Implicit in the narrative are values which form the
core of any style of life or worldview.

For the narrator, and presumably for some of the people of his time, it was reasonable to expect to encounter God through the events of daily living, even for an "unbeliever" like the Pharaoh whose dreams proved a medium for divine communication. Nature is, for the writer, the context of life, and its rhythms and forces are observed, reflected upon, and respected. The natural cycle of plenty and famine is taken for granted. Yet, while there is no thought of attempting to shape nature according to human convenience, stewarding the plentiful resources is seen as a rational approach to surviving in leaner times. The economic system devised by Joseph assumes the value of equitable distribution of limited food, even to those outside the nation where it was grown.

In the view of the storyteller, no dichotomy exists between spiritual and material dimensions of the world. While Joseph's wisdom is enhanced by his communion with God, it is a wisdom that informs decisions and shapes relationships in everyday life. There is also no division between action and vision, for the social designs and governmental institutions are devised as an effective buffer between world forces and people's needs. Similarly, in the person of Joseph, government and public authority are based on a devotion to the common good, rather than standing over against the governed (even if some farmers may have resented giving up twenty percent of their produce to form the food reserve!).

A coherent world view and lifestyle are evident in Genesis 41. It is a view which includes the entire created order as community. Take a few minutes to compare the narrator's assumptions with your own.

Chapter 12

And Furthermore . . .

by David Crean

This book was not designed to show *how* to change lifestyles but *why* we should be developing a lifestyle based less on the ethics of consumption and more on the ethics of responsible stewardship. We are, of course, constantly changing our lifestyles. We are encouraged to. It is so easy to fall into the trap of believing that the new car or whatever will bring convenience, happiness, respect, or whatever other bait may be dangled before us.

The converse is also true. It is hard to adapt to a life of creative simplicity. All societal pressures militate against it. In fact, it may even engender hatred and charges of subversion. "My brothers, do not be surprised if the world hates you. We for our part have crossed over from death to life; this we know because we love our brothers." (I John 3:13–14).

Accordingly, we present a synopsis developed by Jørgen Lissner of the Lutheran World Federation which encapsulates perfectly reasons for lifestyle change that we find cogent.

TEN REASONS FOR SIMPLICITY

Today's global realities call for comfortable Christians to review their lifestyle. Guidelines for a simpler style of life cannot be laid down in universal rules; they must be developed by individuals and communities according to their own imagination and situation. A simpler lifestyle is not a panacea. It may be embarked upon for the wrong reasons, e.g., out of guilt, as a substitute for political action, or in a quest for moral purity. But it can also be meaningful and significant in some or all of the following ways:

1. As an *act of faith* performed for the sake of personal integrity and as an expression of a personal commitment to a more equitable distribution of the world's resources.

2. As an *act of self-defense* against the mind-and-body-polluting effects of overconsumption.

3. As an *act of withdrawal* from the achievement neurosis of our high-pressure, materialist societies.

4. As an *act of solidarity* with the majority of human kind, which has no choice about lifestyle.

5. As an *act of sharing* with others what has been given to us, or of returning what was usurped by us through unjust social and economic structures.

6. As an *act of celebration* of the riches found in creativity, spirituality, and community with others, rather than in mindless materialism.

7. As an *act of provocation* (ostentatious *under*-consumption) to arouse curiosity leading to dialog with others about affluence, alienation, poverty, and social injustice.

8. As an *act of anticipation* of the era when the self-confidence and assertiveness of the underprivileged forces new power relationships and new patterns of resource allocation upon us.

9. As an *act of advocacy* of legislated changes in present patterns of production and consumption, in the direction of a new international economic order.

10. As an *exercise of purchasing power* to redirect production away from the satisfaction of artificially created wants, toward the supplying of goods and services that meet genuine social needs.

The adoption of a simpler lifestyle is meaningful and justifiable for any or all of the above reasons *alone,* regardless of whether it benefits the underprivileged. Demands for "proof of effectiveness" in helping the poor simply bear witness to the myth that "they the poor" are the problem, and "we the rich" have a solution. Yet, if adopted on a large scale, a simpler lifestyle will have significant socio-political side effects both in the rich and in the poor parts of the world. The two most important side effects are likely to be economic and structural adjustments and release of new resources and energies for social change.

Covenants

We would warn those about to embark seriously on a program of lifestyle changes that it should involve a group and lead to development of a community. The formation of such a community might involve joining together in a mutual pledge or covenant.

One such is the Shakertown Pledge. This is brief and covers the points that any such pledge involves.

SHAKERTOWN PLEDGE

Recognizing that the earth and the fulness thereof is a gift from our gracious God, and that we are called to cherish, nurture, and provide loving stewardship for the earth's resources, and recognizing that life itself is a gift, and a call to responsibility, joy, and celebration, I make the following declarations:

1. I declare myself to be a world citizen.

2. I commit myself to lead an ecologically sound life.

3. I commit myself to lead a life of creative simplicity and to share my personal wealth with the world's poor.

4. I commit myself to join with others in the reshaping of institutions in order to bring about a more just global society in which all people have full access to the needed resources for their physical, emotional, intellectual, and spiritual growth.

5. I commit myself to occupational accountability, and so doing I will seek to avoid the creation of products which cause harm to others.

6. I affirm the gift of my body and commit myself to its proper nourishment and physical well-being.

7. I commit myself to examine continually my relations with others, and to attempt to relate honestly, morally, and lovingly to those around me.

8. I commit myself to personal renewal through prayer, meditation, and study.

9. I commit myself to responsible participation in a community of faith.

Study groups would do well to design their own pledge based on the above model. Some may choose to examine the Common Discipline of the Community of the Cross of Nails.

Resources

In the journey to a simpler lifestyle, we need resources to help us on our way—books, audiovisual aids, and organizations. The trouble is that in this area there is a plethora of materials—good, bad, and indifferent—that bewilders and confuses rather than instructs. We have tried to assemble a selection which we believe to be of value.

Books

There are many of these. Among those that need to be studied are those which give the BACKGROUND to the crisis.

Some of these are factual:

The Global 2000 Report to the President was prepared by the Council on Environmental Quality and the Department of State in 1980. It suffers from two disadvantages—dwelling overly on the gloomy problems without suggesting solutions and stopping at the year 2000. However, it is authoritative and provides good reference material (Volume 1, The Summary Report S/N 041-011-00037-8; $3.50 from Superintendent of Documents, U.S. Government Printing Office, Washington, DC 20402).

North-South: A Program for Survival (The Brandt Commission Report), The Independent Commission on International Development Issues, MIT Press, Cambridge, Massachusetts, 1980. This presents a balanced view of the global crisis and the steps that can or should be taken to deal with it. Perhaps rather long and detailed for most, it is, nevertheless, an important reference book.

Three other books are classics of their kind:

The Closing Circle by Barry Commoner (Bantam Books, New York, NY, 1971) first drew attention to the dimensions of the impending ecological crisis and is still worth reading.

Diet for a Small Planet (new edition) by Frances Moore Lappé (Ballantine Books, New York, NY, 1971) gives practical guidelines for responsible diet.

The Twenty Ninth Day by Lester R. Brown (W. W. Norton, New York, NY, 1978) examines global dimensions of the problem.

Many writers have examined the crisis and both described the crisis and developed a PHILOSOPHICAL BASIS for dealing with it.

These are more discursive in style and do not put forth concrete ideas. Nevertheless, in dealing with the future, we need to be aware of writers who have evolved creative ideas about it.

Small Is Beautiful: Economics as if People Mattered by E. F. Schumacher (Perennial Library, Harper and Row, New York, NY, 1973) is, quite simply, a classic and should be required reading for all concerned about present trends.

Creating Alternative Futures by Hazel Henderson (Perigee Books, G. P. Putnam's, New York, NY, 1978) is a collection of essays by a brilliant, articulate, and perceptive writer.

Good Work by E. F. Schumacher (Harper and Row, New York, NY, 1979) was published posthumously and is notable for its common-sense approach.

Christians should be concerned about the theological implications of the present crisis and our steps to rectify the problems with which we live. Accordingly, the following books on THEOLOGY are recommended:

Enough is Enough by John V. Taylor (Augsburg Publishing House, Minneapolis, MN, 1977) is, quite simply, a classic. Chapters 3 and 4 ("The Theology of Enough" and "The Cheerful Revolution") are in and of themselves sufficient reason to invest in the book.

No More Plastic Jesus by Adam Daniel Finnerty (Orbis Books, Maryknoll, NY, 1977) provides a ringing call for a rejection of material values. It may be too radical for some tastes.

Rich Christians in an Age of Hunger by Ronald J. Sider (Paulist Press, New York, NY, 1977) is on its way to becoming a classic. The second section, "A Biblical Perspective on the Poor and Possessions" is especially noteworthy and important.

The Predicament of the Prosperous by Bruce C. Birch and Larry L. Rasmussen (The Westminster Press, Philadelphia, PA, 1978) is useful, especially for putting personal perspectives in the context of global concerns.

Agenda for Biblical People by Jim Wallis (Harper and Row, New York, NY 1976) is also useful. Wallis is founder of the Sojourners Community and develops many of his ideas in this book.

Living More Simply edited by Ronald J. Sider (Inter-Varsity Press, Downer's Grove, IL, 1980) is a series of papers arising out of a conference on lifestyle. It is somewhat uneven but contains two brilliant essays by Peter Davids and Frank Gaebelein on the biblical call for lifestyle simplification.

Two other books examine particular aspects of lifestyle and form a series of which this book is a part: *The Prometheus Question* edited by Charles A. Cesaretti (Seabury Press, New York, NY, 1980) which deals with energy and *Let The Earth Bless The Lord* edited by Charles A. Cesaretti and Stephen K. Commins (Seabury Press, New York, NY, 1981) which deals with land use.

Finally, it is necessary to have TOOLS to cope with changing one's lifestyle. Outstanding in this area is:
The Next Whole Earth Catalog edited by Stewart Brand (Point, 1980; distributed by Random House, Inc., New York, NY). This needs to be in every parish library.

More condensed, perhaps, are:
99 Ways to a Simple Lifestyle edited by Albert J. Fritsch and a team from Center for Science in the Public Interest (Anchor Books, Doubleday, Garden City, NY, 1977).
Living More with Less by Doris Janzen Longacre (Herald Press, Scottsdale, PA, 1980) is compiled from the experiences of Mennonite missionaries. Doris died of cancer before it could be published.
Appropriate Technology Sourcebook, Volumes I and II edited by Ken Darrow and Rick Pam (Volunteers in Asia, Box 4543, Stanford, CA 94305) is full of creative ideas for small-scale projects as well as additional resources.

Two excellent guides for intentional lifestyle change are: *A Guide to Cooperative Alternatives in America* ($5.50 from Communities Publications Cooperative, Box 426, Louise, VA 23093) and *The Energy and Environment Checklist: An Annotated Bibliography of Resources* ($5.55 from Friends of the Earth, 124 Spear Street, San Francisco, CA 94105). Why not get these for your church's library?

There is an amazing abundance of cookbooks. We have selected two:
Future Food by Colin Tudge (Harmony Books, New York, NY 1980).
Cooking with Conscience by Alice Benjamin and Harriet Corrigan (Vineyard Books, Noroton, CT, 1975).

Both have been tested in the crucible of the kitchens of experienced cooks. Both work.

A good, concise book on gardening is:

Gardening with Conscience by Marny Smith (Seabury Press, New York, NY, 1981).

Finally, there are several CURRICULA for further study.

Repairing Christian Lifestyle by Steve Clapp, Sue Brownfield, and Julie Seibert (Council on Ministries, 1211 North Park, P. O. Box 2050, Bloomington, IL 61701, 1980) is a six-session manual for youth.

Lifestyle Change for Children by Doris Lee Shettel (available from United Presbyterian Church, U.S.A., 475 Riverside Drive, New York, NY 10115, $3.50), while structured for children, is also suitable for intergenerational use.

Covenant Group for Lifestyle Assessment by William E. Gibson (revised and enlarged edition, 1981, is available from United Presbyterian Church, U.S.A., 475 Riverside Drive, New York, NY, 10115, $4.00). A revision of a very popular and excellent twelve-session adult curriculum, it is useful for groups who have decided to make a serious commitment to exploring lifestyles.

Audiovisuals

There is, once more, an almost embarrassing abundance of these. The best single source we found is Bullfrog Films, Oley, PA, 19547 (Telephone 215/779-8226).

Noteworthy among their selections are:

"Living the Good Life" (30 minute film, 1977)

"Toast" (12 minute film, 1974)

"Earthbread" (20 minute film, 1973)

"A Sense of Humus" (28 minute film, 1976)

"Looking for Organic America" (28 minute film, 1972)

"Native Self-Reliance" (20 minute filmstrip, 1980)

Perhaps the most provocative film we have seen is the excellent short cartoon film:

"More" (3 minute film, 1974. Obtainable free from Church World Service/CROP, P. O. Box 968, Elkhart, IN, 46514. 219/264-3102). This is suitable for children, as is:

"Supergoop" (30 minute film. Obtainable from Churchill Films, 662 North Robertson Boulevard, Los Angeles, CA, 90069).

Organizations and Journals

Several organizations exist which promote lifestyle simplification. These include:

Alternatives is a not-for-profit organization to help persons interested in voluntary simplicity take charge of their own lives. They publish a newsletter, a Celebration Planning Calendar, and a Christmas Packet among other things. (Alternatives Resource Center, P. O. Box 1707, Forest Park, GA, 30050).

The Other Side is a magazine published monthly by Jubilee, Inc., 300 West Apsley Street, Philadelphia, PA, 19144. (Telephone: 215/849-2178).

Sojourners is a magazine published monthly by the international community, Sojourners Fellowship, 1309 L Street, N.W., Washington, DC, 20005. (Telephone: 202/737-2780). It contains theological reflections and articles on Christian commitment in a tormented world.

Notes

Introduction
1. Frances Moore Lappé, *Diet for a Small Planet* (New York: Ballantine Books, Inc., 1971), pp. 5–6.
2. Richard Grossman and Gail Daneker, *Energy, Jobs and the Economy* (Boston: Alyson Publications, Inc., 1979), p. 47.

Chapter 2
1. Herman E. Daly, ed., *Toward a Steady-State Economy* (San Francisco: Freeman Publishers, 1973).
2. *The Contrasumers: A Citizen's Guide to Resource Conservation* (New York: Praeger Publishers, 1974).
3. For much more detailed illustrations drawn from people's experiences, see Doris Jansen Longacre, *Living More with Less* (Scottdale, PA: Herald Press, 1980). It is an excellent compendium of people's experiences in living more with less. Doris did not care much for the term "lifestyle." To her it seemed something too transient and superficial. She preferred the term "life standard," believing that it caught up more of the idea of timeless values and commitments. Whereas we have used two basic "standards" for lifestyles' concern in this essay (concern for people and the environment), she has broken them down into five: "do justice," "learn from the world community," "nurture people," "cherish the natural order," and "nonconform freely." In that half of the book which is a collection of experiences, she put a symbol in the margin to explain which standard she felt that particular experience illustrated.

Chapter 3
1. *The Book of Common Prayer* (New York: The Church Hymnal Corporation and the Seabury Press, 1979), p. 429.
2. Owen Barfield, *Saving the Appearances: A Study in Idolatry* (New York: Harcourt, Brace, Jovanovich, 1965), p. 15.
3. *Book of Common Prayer*, p. 372.
4. Ibid., p. 372.
5. Matthew Fox, *A Spirituality Named Compassion, and the Healing of the Global Village, Humpty Dumpty and Us* (Minneapolis, MN: Winston Press), p. 36.
6. Marion J. Hatchett, *Commentary on the American Prayer Book* (New York: Seabury Press, 1980).

Chapter 6
1. *Environmental Quality—1980*, The Eleventh Annual Report of the Council on Environmental Quality (Washington, D.C.: Superintendent of Documents, Government Printing Office, 1980), p. 356.
2. *The Washington Post*, 18 January 1981, p. A16. A detailed discussion of this problem is found in *Environmental Quality—1980*, pp. 348–360.
3. *The Washington Spectator*, 15 May 1980, p. 1.
4. Janet Marinelli, "Eco-crime on the Equator," *Environmental Action*, March 1980, p. 7.

Chapter 7
1. T.S. Eliot, Choruses from "The Rock," *Collected Poems 1909–1962* (New York: Harcourt, Brace, and World, 1970).
2. Ibid.
3. Barbara W. Tuchman, "Picture of Perfection," *New York Times Magazine*, 2 November 1980.
4. Wendell Berry, "A Secular Pilgrimage," *A Continuous Harmony* (New York: Harcourt Brace Jovanovich, 1975), p. 10.
5. Harrison Brown, *The Human Future Revisited* (New York: W.W. Norton, 1978).
6. Barry Commoner, *The Closing Circle* (New York: Bantam Books, 1971). (See especially chapter 9, "The Technological Flaw").
7. Donella H. Meadows, Dennis L. Meadows, Jorgen Randes, and

William W. Behrens III, *The Limits to Growth,* 2nd ed. (New York: Signet Books, The New American Library, 1972), p. 156.
8. Ibid., pp. 157−158.
9. William Shakespeare, *Hamlet,* act 3, sc. 1, lines 57−60.
10. Meadows, et al., *Limits to Growth,* p. 158.
11. Hazel Henderson, *Creating Alternative Futures* (New York: G.P. Putnam, Perigee Books, 1978), p. 402.
12. Ibid.
13. Ibid., p. 366 for a more comprehensive list.
14. Je n'avais pas besoin de cette hypothèse-là.
15. Berry, *Continuous Harmony,* p. 8.

Chapter 9
1. Doris Janzen Longacre, *Living More With Less* (Scottdale, Pennsylvania: Herald Press, 1980), p. 17.
2. Doris Janzen Longacre, *Living More With Less Cookbook* (Scottdale, Pennsylvania: Herald Press, 1976).

Contributors

Bruce C. Birch is Professor of Old Testament Studies at Wesley Theological Seminary, Washington, D.C. He is coauthor (with Larry Rasmussen) of *The Predicament of the Prosperous*.

Richard A. Bower is Associate Rector of Trinity Episcopal Church, Princeton, New Jersey. He has authored *Adult Learning and the Catechism* and has developed music for Rite II of the Episcopal *Book of Common Prayer*.

Preston Browning is Professor of English at the University of Illinois at Chicago Circle. He is also on the staff of World Hunger Education Service, Washington, D.C.

David Crean is Staff Officer for Hunger for the Episcopal Church. He was formerly on the faculty of the College of Agriculture, The Ohio State University.

Sister Dorcas, C.S.M., and *Nancy Wabshaw* are with the DeKoven Foundation for Church Work in Racine, Wisconsin. Nancy is a postulant in the Community of Saint Mary.

Eric and Helen Ebbeson are members of the National Hunger Committee of the Episcopal Church. Eric is a retired engineer and Helen is an education consultant. They live in Rye, New Hampshire where they are working on practical methods for a simpler, more creative lifestyle.

Gary T. Evans is consultant in religious education to the Episcopal Diocese of Northern Michigan and is also a free-lance consultant in adult education.

Charlotte Fardelmann is a free-lance journalist from Portsmouth, New Hampshire. She has published widely in such journals as *The Christian Science Monitor* and in religious newspapers.

David Dodson-Gray is co-director, with his wife, Elizabeth, of the Bolton Institute for a Sustainable Future, Boston, Massachusetts. They are graduates of Yale Divinity School. The Institute is a "think tank" concerned with issues raised by the transition to a sustainable society.

Milo Shannon-Thornberry is director of Alternatives in Forest Park, Georgia. He was associated with the development of the WHEAT Program of the National Council of Churches.

David V. Williams is Associate Professor of Psychology at Ithaca College and a partner in OmniCom Associates, Ithaca, New York. He is a consultant and researcher in nonverbal communication and communication environments, especially in the context of intentional community.